A Celebration of Poets

WEST
GRADES K-3
SPRING 2012

A Celebration of Poets
West
Grades K-3
Spring 2012

An anthology compiled by Creative Communication, Inc.

Published by:

PO BOX 303 • SMITHFIELD, UTAH 84335
TEL. 435-713-4411 • WWW.POETICPOWER.COM

All rights reserved. No part of this book may be reproduced or transmitted in any form or by any means, electronic or mechanical without written permission of the author and publisher.

Copyright © 2012 by Creative Communication, Inc.
Printed in the United States of America

ISBN: 978-1-60050-522-5

Foreword

Dear Reader:

Is writing meaningful to your life? The greatest gift that my mother ever gave me was her writing. For over 70 years, she kept a record of every moment that was meaningful in her life. Taking these stories, she created several books which allow me to remember and relive moments in my childhood and the life my mother had as she grew up. She got into the habit of writing and has now left a great legacy.

As a parent, I know that my children bring home samples of their writing from school assignments each week. However, after a few days on the school bulletin board or fridge at home, these slices of their lives often get thrown away.

The books we publish create a legacy for each of these students. Their work is recorded to show friends, family and future generations. We are glad to be part of capturing their thoughts, hopes and dreams.

The students that are published have shared a bit of themselves with us. Thank you for being part of this process, as every writer needs a reader. We hope that by recognizing these students, writing will become a part of their life and bring meaning to others.

Sincerely,

Thomas Worthen, Ph.D.
Editor
Creative Communication

WRITING CONTESTS!

Enter our next POETRY contest!
Enter our next ESSAY contest!

Why should I enter?
Win prizes and get published! Each year thousands of dollars in prizes are awarded throughout North America. The top writers in each division receive a monetary award and a free book that includes their published poem or essay. Entries of merit are also selected to be published in our anthology.

Who may enter?
There are four divisions in the poetry contest. The poetry divisions are grades K-3, 4-6, 7-9, and 10-12. There are three divisions in the essay contest. The essay divisions are grades 3-6, 7-9, and 10-12.

What is needed to enter the contest?
To enter the poetry contest send in one original poem, 21 lines or less. To enter the essay contest send in one original non-fiction essay, 250 words or less, on any topic. Each entry must include the student's name, grade, address, city, state, and zip code, and the student's school name and school address. Students who include their teacher's name may help their teacher qualify for a free copy of the anthology. Contest changes and updates are listed at www.poeticpower.com.

How do I enter?
Enter a poem online at:
www.poeticpower.com
or
Mail your poem to:
   Poetry Contest
   PO Box 303
   Smithfield, UT 84335

Enter an essay online at:
www.poeticpower.com
or
Mail your essay to:
   Essay Contest
   PO Box 303
   Smithfield, UT 84335

When is the deadline?
Poetry contest deadlines are December 6th, April 4th and August 19th. Essay contest deadlines are October 18th, February 19th and July 15th. Students can enter one poem and one essay for each spring, summer, and fall contest deadline.

Are there benefits for my school?
Yes. We award $12,500 each year in grants to help with Language Arts programs. Schools qualify to apply for a grant by having 15 or more accepted entries.

Are there benefits for my teacher?
Yes. Teachers with five or more students published receive a free anthology that includes their students' writing.

For more information please go to our website at
www.poeticpower.com,
email us at editor@poeticpower.com or call 435-713-4411.

Page iv

TABLE OF CONTENTS

POETIC ACHIEVEMENT HONOR SCHOOLS 1

LANGUAGE ARTS GRANT RECIPIENTS 5

GRADES K-1-2-3 HIGH MERIT POEMS 7

INDEX 155

STATES INCLUDED IN THIS EDITION:

ALASKA
ARIZONA
CALIFORNIA
HAWAII
IDAHO
MONTANA
NEVADA
NEW MEXICO
OREGON
TEXAS
WASHINGTON
WYOMING

Spring 2012 Poetic Achievement Honor Schools

* Teachers who had fifteen or more poets accepted to be published

The following schools are recognized as receiving a "Poetic Achievement Award." This award is given to schools who have a large number of entries of which over fifty percent are accepted for publication. With hundreds of schools entering our contest, only a small percent of these schools are honored with this award. The purpose of this award is to recognize schools with excellent Language Arts programs. This award qualifies these schools to receive a complimentary copy of this anthology. In addition, these schools are eligible to apply for a Creative Communication Language Arts Grant. Grants of two hundred and fifty dollars each are awarded to further develop writing in our schools.

A E Arnold Elementary School
Cypress, CA
    Jean Chen-Wu*
    Janice Wright*

Anna Marie Jacobson Elementary School
Chandler, AZ
    Kathi McNeeley*

Annunciation Orthodox School
Houston, TX
    Mrs. Hopper
    Lise Lanceley*
    Christy Naponic*
    Kiki Przewlocki*
    Mrs. Thurber

CLASS Academy
Portland, OR
    Cortney Benvenuto
    Heather Kinlin
    Heather Marr
    Nicholas McLean*
    Ashley Scuderi

Edward Byrom Elementary School
Tualatin, OR
    Bruce Bowman*

Fir Grove Elementary School
Roseburg, OR
    Debra Allen*

Gause Elementary School
Washougal, WA
    Mrs. Taie
    Connie Vernon*

A Celebration of Poets – West Grades K-3 Spring 2012

Greenleaf Elementary School
Oakland, CA
 Tai Amri*

H W Schulze Elementary School
San Antonio, TX
 Cara Rakowitz*

Horn Academy
Bellaire, TX
 Lisa Miller*

Islamic School of Muslim
Educational Trust
Portland, OR
 Jennifer Al-Araby
 Katie Escobar
 Vi Pham*

Islamic School of San Diego
San Diego, CA
 Aisha Boulil*
 Tamador Elyoussef
 Fardusa Sharif*
 Munira Vazeer

Kentwood Elementary School
Los Angeles, CA
 Roberta Guarnieri*

Keone'ula Elementary School
Ewa Beach, HI
 Aimee K. Matsuura*
 Lindsey Richards*

Laurence School
Valley Glen, CA
 Judy Braun
 Merrie Libicki
 Kim Milman

Laurence School (cont.)
Valley Glen, CA
 Steve Nairin
 Rochelle Robinson
 Wendy Wolin

Legacy Christian Academy
Alamogordo, NM
 Theresa Bean
 Yvonne Horgan*
 Mrs. Molander
 Mrs. Scott
 Mrs. Smith
 Christina Stewart

Lolo Elementary School
Lolo, MT
 Jennifer Christensen*

McDowell Mountain Elementary
School
Fountain Hills, AZ
 Jennifer Harley*
 Talia Houseal
 Linda Ness*
 Madeleine Smith*

Meadows Elementary School
El Centro, CA
 Mary Aubrey
 Patricia Beckett
 Rosa Cruz
 Cheryl Rodriguez

Medina Elementary School
Medina, WA
 Teresa Gibbs
 Kristi Stroyan*

Poetic Achievement Honor Schools

Mesa Vista Elementary School
El Paso, TX
Mrs. Matta
Frances Padilla*
Mrs. Rivera

Midland Elementary School
Moreno Valley, CA
Debbie Eytcheson*

Nenahnezad Community School
Fruitland, NM
Jana Begay
Mrs. Joe*
Mrs. Ramone-Wilson

New Horizon School LA Campus
Los Angeles, CA
Nabeeha Aleem
Nishat Alikhan
Sana Suzuki

Robert L Stevens Elementary School
Santa Rosa, CA
Amber Lesset*

Scholars Academy
San Jose, CA
Shailaja Nayak*

South Bosque Elementary School
Waco, TX
Mrs. Ashenfelter*
Mrs. Cates

Spring Valley Elementary School
Hewitt, TX
Emilee Ashenfelter*
Kathy Tomecek

St Helen Catholic School
South Gate, CA
Ms. Morales
Bernadette Windsor*

St John's Episcopal Day School
McAllen, TX
Beverly Moore*

St Joseph Catholic School
Auburn, CA
Charlotte Corkery
Kristen Mendonsa*
Gayle Moore
Marie Piñon
Therese Rozowski
Georgia Stempel
Mira Wordelman
Jamie Zalud

St Peter Prince of Apostles School
San Antonio, TX
Katherine Trimble*

The Mirman School
Los Angeles, CA
Dr. Julia Candace Corliss*
Wendy Samson*
Mr. Wiener
Marjorie Zinman

The Presentation School
Sonoma, CA
Moya Jones-Neely*

Top Kids Center
Monrovia, CA
Kimberly Gauthier
Gilbert Mendez

A Celebration of Poets – West Grades K-3 Spring 2012

Tracy Learning Center - Primary
  Charter School
    Tracy, CA
      Beth Christensen
      Jenna Lins*
      Lori Rodieck
      Carolyn Woods

Wilchester Elementary School
  Houston, TX
    Mrs. Hay
    Stacy Morgan*
    Kristie Shankles*

Woodcrest School
  Tarzana, CA
    Mrs. Idolor
    Mrs. Martin*
    Luanne Paglione*
    Michelle Tran*

Woodway Elementary School
  Waco, TX
    Mrs. Ashenfelter*

Ygnacio Valley Christian School
  Concord, CA
    Diane Oatis*

Language Arts Grant Recipients 2011-2012

After receiving a "Poetic Achievement Award" schools are encouraged to apply for a Creative Communication Language Arts Grant. The following is a list of schools who received a two hundred and fifty dollar grant for the 2011-2012 school year.

Annapolis Royal Regional Academy, Annapolis Royal, NS
Bear Creek Elementary School, Monument, CO
Bellarmine Preparatory School, Tacoma, WA
Birchwood School, Cleveland, OH
Bluffton Middle School, Bluffton, SC
Brookville Intermediate School, Brookville, OH
Butler High School, Augusta, GA
Carmi-White County High School, Carmi, IL
Classical Studies Academy, Bridgeport, CT
Coffee County Central High School, Manchester, TN
Country Hills Elementary School, Coral Springs, FL
Coyote Valley Elementary School, Middletown, CA
Emmanuel-St Michael Lutheran School, Fort Wayne, IN
Excelsior Academy, Tooele, UT
Great Meadows Middle School, Great Meadows, NJ
Holy Cross High School, Delran, NJ
Kootenay Christian Academy, Cranbrook, BC
LaBrae Middle School, Leavittsburg, OH
Ladoga Elementary School, Ladoga, IN
Mater Dei High School, Evansville, IN
Palmer Catholic Academy, Ponte Vedra Beach, FL
Pine View School, Osprey, FL
Plato High School, Plato, MO

Language Arts Grant Winners cont.

Rivelon Elementary School, Orangeburg, SC
Round Lake High School, Round Lake, MN
Sacred Heart School, Oxford, PA
Shadowlawn Elementary School, Green Cove Springs, FL
Starmount High School, Boonville, NC
Stevensville Middle School, Stevensville, MD
Tadmore Elementary School, Gainesville, GA
Trask River High School, Tillamook, OR
Vacaville Christian Schools, Vacaville, CA
Wattsburg Area Middle School, Erie, PA

Grades K-1-2-3 Top Ten Winners

List of Top Ten Winners for Grades K-3; listed alphabetically

Leora Baumgarten, Grade 3
Yeshiva at the Jersey Shore, NJ

Addison Boehme, Grade 3
College Park School, SK

Jason Brooks, Grade 3
Washington West Elementary School, NY

Amelia Duerkop, Grade 3
Poplar Bridge Elementary School, MN

Veronica Lucius, Grade 3
German International School Boston, MA

Alyssa Noseworthy, Grade 3
Longfellow Elementary School, WI

Aaron Peng, Grade 2
Dodson Elementary School, MI

Olivia Randle, Grade 3
College Gate Elementary School, AK

Justin Wright, Grade 2
Walsh Elementary School, CO

Sydney Wu, Grade 2
Memorial Elementary School, NJ

All Top Ten Poems can be read at www.poeticpower.com

Note: The Top Ten poems were finalized through an online voting system. Creative Communication's judges first picked out the top poems. These poems were then posted online. The final step involved thousands of students and teachers who registered as the online judges and voted for the Top Ten poems. We hope you enjoy these selections.

Jordin

S ea is very dangerous for people.
O xygen is what people breathe.
M ayor is a person who gives speeches.
E arth is a ball of life.
R eading gives us knowledge.
S mart is when someone knows everything.
A merica is where we live.
U nderstand is when you know something.
L earning is what you do in class.
T hinking is learning.
E xperiment is building.
D octor is a person that takes care of you.

Jordin Bailey, Grade 3
Midland Elementary School, CA

Until the Sun Went Up

I was an ice cream
Until the sun went up
I was soft and cold
Until the sun went up
I was shining and wet
Until the sun went up
I was squishy and delicate
Until the sun went up
I was mushy and freezing
Until the sun went up
I was beautiful and icy
And still the sun came up

Sharad Krishnan, Grade 3
Anna Marie Jacobson Elementary School, AZ

The Sky

At sunrise, the sun rises.
It glimmers at me in the daytime.
At sunset, the sun begins to disappear.
Shortly after, the stars cover the sky like a sheet of paper.
Another friend appears in the sky, the moon.
The planets join the night parades.
Oh! Such a beauty to observe.
The sky is my best friend because it goes with me everywhere.
I love the sky.

Ayoub Toumi, Grade 3
Islamic School of San Diego, CA

High Merit Poems – Grades K, 1, 2, and 3

Aggies

Aggies Aggies hear them roaring
That's because Ryan Tannehill's scoring
With Ryan Swope on his back
UT's under attack
Aggies will win and do it all again
UT's sure to lose because of all the boos
Aggies Aggies fight fight fight
Aggies will win day and night
Caroline Dina, Grade 3
Wilchester Elementary School, TX

Flying

I wish I could fly
Only if I could fly
It would be better
Then I could be like a bird
But not like a herd or a rock
But like a flock
If someone could fly and I couldn't
I would die
Jonathan Daniel Horton, Grade 3
Wilchester Elementary School, TX

Trains

Mr. F1 car is in a race
I can barely see his face
He's red and blue choo choo!
Racing around the track is
What he's trying to do
My favorite trains are gas turbines!
They're powerful and change at times
My dad and I shop for them online!
Craig Thilgen, Grade 1
Hadley School, CA

Jell-o

Dancing like Jell-o in the kids' heads
How many Jell-o can you find?
Banana Jell-o, ice cream Jell-o,
Strawberry Jell-o,
Green and white Jell-o.
Brianna Martinez, Kindergarten
Legacy Christian Academy, NM

Springtime

In the spring it is sunny,
The bears come out, and that's not funny.

In the spring, there are allergies,
There are lots of evergreen trees.

In the spring flowers bloom,
The caterpillars just consume.

A squirrel climbs up the trees,
When someone comes, it just flees.

In the spring, I play basketball,
On the court, you can fall.

In the spring, I plant flowers,
Other things help, like rain showers.

In the spring I read books,
Some of them are judged by their looks.

In the spring I drink lots of water,
Just in case, it gets hotter.
Rohan Bhansali, Grade 3
Woodcrest School, CA

This Is Mine

This is my cat
Her name is Lulu
She is black and brown
She is not cuckoo

This is my cat
She is really smart
She is not an outdoor cat
She doesn't drive a cart

This is my cat
She can open a door
She can turn on a faucet
She doesn't go under the floor
Torin Perkins, Grade 2
CLASS Academy, OR

A Celebration of Poets – West Grades K-3 Spring 2012

My Friend
My friend
She is very nice
She has blonde hair
She is beautiful
She has blue eyes
She plays
With me
She does art
Her name is Alex
Sage Canon, Grade 1
Horn Academy, TX

Snowflakes
Snowflakes,
Snowflakes falling to the ground
Snowflakes,
Snowflakes are always white.
Snowflakes,
Snowflakes so glittery
Snowflakes,
Snowflakes are so fun to play with.
I love snowflakes!
Alexis Bartley, Grade 2
Horn Academy, TX

Coco
Coco is very cute
Pawing, pouncing, leaping
Basking in the sun,
Having so much fun!
Tumbling as she runs
Starting to slow down,
As night comes she gets very quiet
And sleeps as the wind moves swiftly
Upon Coco's fur
Kate Bolger, Grade 3
Horn Academy, TX

I Love
I love my puppy
Named
Pancake
He jumps on
My face
I love my sister
Because
She takes care
of me
Kevin Rodriguez, Grade 1
Horn Academy, TX

Lady Friend
My lady friend is so sweet,
The first time we met she was wonderful,
I have not proposed yet, but I am scared,
I try to prepare, but I just can't do it,
We are each as gentle as a dove,
But we just literally fell in love.
Sydney Brooksby, Grade 3
Edward Byrom Elementary School, OR

Flowers
When flowers are born
They're closed real tight
But then they grow
And their petals
Shine in the
Light
Ella Jeffries, Grade 2
Seattle Jewish Community School, WA

Horse
Horse
Fun, happy
Prancing, whinnying, running
Riding ponies is exciting
Pinto
Jazmin Barnes, Grade 3
Ygnacio Valley Christian School, CA

PSP
I got a new touch screen PSP.
It's got 3,000,000,000 megabytes
It's the finest PSP in the world.
It's got the best games in the world.
Then one night, we got bored
Kylen Love, Grade 2
Whatcom Discovery School, WA

High Merit Poems – Grades K, 1, 2, and 3

Babies
good,
nice,
soft,
smooth,
squishy,
cute,
adorable,
funny,
wild,
loud,
noisy,
hitter,
terror,
cries.
Will Whitton, Grade 3
Wilchester Elementary School, TX

Spring
Spring! Spring! Spring is here.
It's a wonderful time of the year.
I like to see critters on the ground.
It's good to have flowers around.
Or maybe have a swim in the ocean
and put on some sun lotion.
I will have fun
and rest in the sun.
I'll go to my cousin's house
and pick up a tiny mouse.
I'll go to the zoo
and pet my dog too.
Spring! Spring! Spring is here.
It's a wonderful time of the year!
Russell Ramos, Grade 1
Woodcrest School, CA

Dinosaur
Dinosaur
Roars
When it's time
to eat at home
It eats people
Austin Palmerton, Kindergarten
Whatcom Discovery School, WA

This Is Me
Angela
Happy, fast, nice
Loves dad
Feels funny
Needs friends
Gives love
Fears the dark
Would like to see a koala
Tolentino
Angela Tolentino, Grade 1
Kentwood Elementary School, CA

My Feelings
Haley
Kind, happy, funny
Loves family
Feels happy
Needs friends
Gives loves
Fears brain freeze
Would like to see Fiji
Prasad
Haley Prasad, Grade 1
Kentwood Elementary School, CA

Halloween
Halloween scary
Halloween fun
Halloween creepy
Halloween spooky
Halloween pumpkins
Halloween!
Dana Malin, Grade 1
Horn Academy, TX

Fire
Here's a fire
There was a lot of fire engines
It was up in the mountains
It burned a lot of houses down
And nobody died
Kody Rathgeber, Kindergarten
Legacy Christian Academy, NM

A Celebration of Poets – West Grades K-3 Spring 2012

Under the Sun

One sunny day,
I asked my mom,
"What should I do?"
Mom said,
"I have an idea for you!"
My mom and I
Played outside.
We played Seek and Hide.
It was a great fun
To play with mom
Under the sun!

Cole Monroe, Grade 2
Westview School, TX

Rock Stars

Rock stars
Cool, nice, and crazy
Laughter, funny, pretty
My class is the rock stars
They're really crazy
Sometimes
Loud music
Sometimes
Soft music
Sometimes
Just the right music!

Cayla Gottesman, Grade 1
Horn Academy, TX

Black

Black is bad like my hamster
Black is like a rocket
Black is like the sky
Black is like a marker
Black tastes like yogurt
Black smells like socks
Black sounds like hard knocking
Black feels like hard rocks
Black looks like dark chocolate
Black makes me scared
Black is dirty

Brett Abitante, Grade 1
Kentwood Elementary School, CA

Sun

The sun,
Hot and fiery
Like phoenixes across
The sky
Seen like
A candle that lights
The way
Seen throughout
The dawn of day
And disappears
Behind a hill

Katherine Chen, Grade 2
Horn Academy, TX

Spring Is Here

Birds fly to the trees,
They also feel the great cool breeze.

Gophers eat your plants all day,
You want them to stay away.

Water flows through the river,
Don't go swimming or you'll shiver.

Kids play in the park,
You can hear the dogs bark.

Joseph Newstadt, Grade 2
Woodcrest School, CA

Summer Seal

S eals play in the water.
U nder the water, seals catch their food.
M other seals play with their pups
M other seas catch their food for the pups.
E very seal eats fish.
R ocks hurt the seals if they touch them.

S pring is when Ben found the seals.
E arly in the morning seals swim.
A t the beach seals swim.
L ots of seals swim far.

Chris Castellano, Grade 3
Midland Elementary School, CA

High Merit Poems – Grades K, 1, 2, and 3

Phenomenal Teachers
Playful and loving
Help and assist you in need
Enjoy, that is all you do with them
Never annoying or angry
Offer fun and exciting times
Many are sweet, comfort you, and are supreme
Excellent at giving kindness
No teacher does this: discourage you
Achieve, that is something they help you do
Lots of laughing and learning

Teachers, they are phenomenal
Encouragement, they don't forget it
And oh, how they inspire
Courage, they give plenty
High quality, there is so much of it
Every day they cheer you on (especially my teacher!)
Really, they give so much knowledge
Support you can't forget

Hana Syed, Grade 2
Aikin Elementary School, TX

Science Class

I have Science Class in 3 minutes.
What am I going to do?

I still don't have a project yet.
What am I going to do?

Should a build the Eiffel Tower out of some string cheese?
Or build a brain out of macaroni which kind of makes me sneeze?

Should I build a super structure out of real cool clay?
Or a super cool model of human's DNA?

I have Science class in 1 minute and I still
don't have a project yet!

Oh no! I'm going to be late.
I think I'm going to faint.

Amelia Jobe, Grade 3
CAPE Charter School, CA

Lollipops
Lollipops!
Delicious lollipops,
Yummy lollipops,
Orange lollipops,
Juicy lollipops,
And crunchy lollipops, too!
I love lollipops, how about you?
Jamie Ponteres, Kindergarten
A E Arnold Elementary School, CA

Lollipops
Lollipops!
Purple lollipops,
Juicy lollipops,
Crunchy lollipops,
Round lollipops,
And grape lollipops, too!
I love lollipops, how about you?
Joelle Ferguson, Kindergarten
A E Arnold Elementary School, CA

Blue
Blue is like blueberries in a bush.
Blue is like fish in the sea.
Blue is like the ocean.
Blue is like the sky.
Blue is like the Earth spinning around.
Blue tastes like blueberries in a bowl.
Blue feels like the waves in the ocean.
Ricardo Banaga, Grade 2
Meadows Union School, CA

Flower
Flower
Pretty and bright
Petals everywhere
Orange and blue
Pink and purple also
Green leaves
Green stems
Mohor Sarkar, Grade 1
Horn Academy, TX

Dolphin
Dolphin
Hawaiian salt water
Swim and splash
And have fun
Eats tuna fish
Collecting shells
Dolphin
Emily Grace Ray, Grade 1
J.G. Johnson Elementary School, NV

The World Around Me
Grass sways,
rabbits hop.
I will never stop looking at the
movements around me.
Frogs jump,
butterflies fly.
I love the world that surrounds me.
Vivian Brittain, Grade 3
Robinson Elementary School, TX

Lollipops
Lollipops!
Purple lollipops,
Sweet lollipops,
Soft lollipops,
Sour lollipops,
And good lollipops, too!
I love lollipops, how about you?
Jimin Cha, Kindergarten
A E Arnold Elementary School, CA

Lollipops
Lollipops!
Gold lollipops,
Sticky lollipops,
Slippery lollipops,
Round lollipops,
and tasty lollipops, too!
I love lollipops, how about you?
Damien Ramali, Kindergarten
A E Arnold Elementary School, CA

Summer Holidays

Hey It's a Summer holiday
Doesn't it make ya wanna laugh and play
Its fun in the sun for June and July
Let your dreams soar and high five the sky

Hey It's a summer holiday
Havin' lots of fun in the month after May

Summer holidays: go for the gold
It's not that easy so just be bold
Playin' basketball n' having fun
All you have to do is run run run
Summer holidays are the best
Always have fun and never rest

Aadithyaa Sridhar Baskari, Grade 3
Fairlands Elementary School, CA

Band

The people singing on the stage
love, romance in the air, party with loud music.

Midnight with sweet magical
merry parties all day with boys and girls.

The music all loud with people singing
rock and roll all night.

The crowd goes wild every day,
dancing to loud music, there is plenty to share.

We're laughing out loud
with our funny friends all night.

Isabel Velasquez, Grade 3
H W Schulze Elementary School, TX

My Golden Retriever Emma

My golden retriever, Emma, is so loving. She
licks me on the lips. Once she licked me 500
times! She could be a licking monkey! When I
run with the ball she tackles me every time
like a football player!

Doug Suell III, Grade 2
Annunciation Orthodox School, TX

Stormy Weather
When the rain crashes down,
It's scary.
Thunder crashes,
Rain splashes,
It's like a bear clawing at you.
Sylvana Guzman, Kindergarten
The Presentation School, CA

Snow Goose
One day a Snow Goose got hungry.
He walked around.
He found a good spot.
He caught a shrew.
He gulped it before you can count to two.
Julian Rich, Grade 2
Troy Elementary School, OR

Flower
It starts with a flower.
Then it takes an hour.
Where are the bees
Oh yeah…
I had to plant the seeds.
Annie Tellez, Grade 3
Wilchester Elementary School, TX

The Sun
The sun's lovely warmth
Smiles down on Earth below,
Warm sleepy-eyed seeds,
Prods them to shed dirt covers,
Awake now, stretching skyward.
Mason Jones, Grade 3
Wilchester Elementary School, TX

Mom
Respectful, friendly
My mom is…
Everything I've asked for.
Something beautiful with green eyes.
Mommy.
Jackson Allred, Grade 3
Wilchester Elementary School, TX

Mouse
Mouse
Small, fast
Loves eating cheese
Scares my mom dearly
Rat
Sam Cohen, Grade 3
Wilchester Elementary School, TX

School
I hear bells ringing
Kids singing
Teachers screaming
I'm definitely
In school!
George Mills, Grade 3
Horn Academy, TX

Camouflage
Camouflage flutter
Beautiful wings
Flutter fast
Beautiful flutter
Camouflage flutter
Vivian Huynh, Grade 2
Horn Academy, TX

A Cinquain of a Hare
Mister
Oh Mister Hare
Oh lazy hare, it is spring
Why do you sleep like an old bear?
Emerge
Mateo Livingstone, Grade 3
Soquel Elementary School, CA

Mutts
Mutts
sweet, good
soft, fluffy, gentle
cute, colorful, playful, fun
bark, sniff, howl, digging, growl
Maria Rojas, Grade 3
Wilchester Elementary School, TX

High Merit Poems – Grades K, 1, 2, and 3

Rainbow

A rainbow is so colorful
Because it is so beautiful.
I love seeing it so much,
That I want to touch.
Bianca Valdivia, Grade 2
St Helen Catholic School, CA

Rainbow

A rainbow is beautiful as you can see.
As you see the wind blowing by the sea.
A sea is great for a rainbow to shine,
But later on it will wear down to a twine.
Melody Zatarain, Grade 2
St Helen Catholic School, CA

Flowers Grow

Flowers grow in the bright light,
But some flowers only glow at night.
The roses get up at noon,
But they will go to sleep soon.
Karina Rangel, Grade 2
St Helen Catholic School, CA

Easter Sunshine

Easter, I love it.
It makes the sunshine come out.
It makes the Easter bunny come out.
It makes the world happy.
Kaylom Austin, Grade 3
Robinson Elementary School, TX

Sunshine

Sunshine sunshine
Give the world light
Make our hearts feel bright
And make us feel light
Jordan Bury, Grade 3
Urie Elementary School, WY

Come with Me to the Savannah

See the cheetahs chase after the gazelle.
Hear the lion roaring at the animals.
Feel the zebra's black hair on it neck.
Smell the fire burning on the grass.
Nicholas Stellino, Grade 3
A E Arnold Elementary School, CA

Monster Truck

A monster truck can jump very high.
A monster truck can go very fast.
Some monster trucks race
And some monster trucks are last.
Braidon Deere, Grade 2
Warren Elementary School, OR

Burning Logs

B urning logs
U nder the stove
R esting in there, awaiting to die
N one survived
Payton Leather, Grade 3
Hidden Hills Elementary School, AZ

Rabbit

Cute, soft
Hopping, jumping, running
Rabbit hops around in the bush.
Bunny
Courtney Matchers, Grade 3
Nenahnezad Community School, NM

Cat

Black, mean
Scratching, biting, eating
A cat is wild and mean.
Kitten
Tisheena Hoskie, Grade 3
Nenahnezad Community School, NM

My Stuffed Bunny
Cute Cuddly,
Nice to sleep with
When I pick it up
It stares at me
I stare at him
Gabriela Rodriguez, Grade 2
Horn Academy, TX

Coral Snake
Something slithers by
You see a pattern of
Red, yellow
It is a
Coral snake
Conor Shanley, Grade 2
Horn Academy, TX

The Buzz
Buzz, Buzz,
there goes a Bee flying around the sky.

Buzz, Buzz,
looking for a flower to land.
Alyzai Cariaso, Grade 2
East Hill Elementary School, WA

Birds
Like to watch birds
Huddle up and fly south
Chirp and chirp they
Find a new
Home
Emily Yu, Grade 2
Horn Academy, TX

Sister
Sister
Happy, younger
Playing, talking, jumping
She is funny to play with
Benedicte
Sebastian Fitjar, Grade 1
Kentwood Elementary School, CA

Fishing
Fishing
Big, wet
Slimy, funny, splashy
Fish are good to eat
Northern Pike
Max Eaton, Grade 3
Valley View Christian School, MT

Flowers
Flowers so pretty, pink, purple, blue,
I love their aroma they're
So beautiful when they bloom
They grow in green grass
I love flowers!
Molly Vestal, Grade 2
Horn Academy, TX

Cousins
My cousins are nice
My cousins are cool
They play with me
My cousins like to race
They are important to me
Rushil Chetty, Grade 1
Horn Academy, TX

Twin
Sydney
Blond, brave
Playing helping, reading
Likes the movie *Lorax*
Sister
Joshua Kazden, Grade 1
Kentwood Elementary School, CA

Quail
Quail can fly oh so very high,
They can jump and peep,
run and sleep.
Quail are cute that's a fact,
Quail are silly and act like that.
Neeley Farnum, Grade 3
Robinson Elementary School, TX

Here's to You

Here's to friends!
The kind people!
Friends!

Here's to the school ones
The very, very cool ones
The itsy bitsy small ones
The play with you tall ones
Oh, I love my friends!

Here's to the kind ones
The good at finding ones
The like to play in mud ones
The best bud ones
Oh, I love my friends!

And here's to you!
The best friend ever!
Yes, You!

Benjamin Dozal, Grade 3
Anna Marie Jacobson Elementary School, AZ

The Pool at the Hotel

When I saw the pool
I said, "This is so cool!"
There were three people I met
but they were already wet.
We went in with a "splash"
It was a splash bash
We're all full of water!
As wet as otters.
It was hot
even in the parking lot!
I loved the breeze.
I could swim with ease.
I ate a hot dog with a bun
in the glazing sun.
We ate chips.
I swam so much I had aching hips.
I went to the room for some shade
The room was so clean I said, "What a great maid!"

Isabella Arevalo, Grade 3
St Anthony Immaculate Conception School, CA

Thunder
Crash,
boom, boom,
Two voices yell,
I'm scared,
I'm not,
Ha! Ha! I hear
the word scared,
I'm not!
You are,
No, you are.
You are wrong.
Am not.
Are too,
Just yell,
What?
Yell for mom,
Ha! Ha! Scared you are,
Yes, okay,
I'm scared.
Jovanni Barragan, Grade 2
Robert L Stevens Elementary School, CA

Baseball
I love to
play baseball.
I will hit a grand slam.
It will be really far,
and I hit a car.
When I pitch I strike
everybody out.
The batter hits a pop fly,
and I catch it —
and it was an out!

It is the last inning 10-10 —
we are tied!
I get up to bat —
2 strikes, 3 balls and
I hit a home run.
We win, Yay!
Tyson Fritze, Grade 3
Robinson Elementary School, TX

Fall
Leaves falling
Having fun
Apples falling from the trees
Jumping in the leaves
Eating pumpkin pie
Spending time
With my family
Grace Kant, Grade 1
Horn Academy, TX

Weird
Weird scary haunted houses,
freaky clowns throwing rocks.
The scary music with frightening drums.

With little scary animals and fake
remote-control silly skeletons.
Fake bodies on the floor.
Nathanial Gonzalez, Grade 3
H W Schulze Elementary School, TX

Soldiers
They walk so much,
They help people in need,
Some use helicopters,
Some do not.
They fight bad guys and,
They keep me safe,
Thank you soldiers.
Aaditya Bhat, Kindergarten
Scholars Academy, CA

Sparkly Diamonds
I like diamonds because they're nice,
I like diamonds because they sparkle,
We can wear diamonds to parties,
We can wear them when we go out,
I love the diamond shape,
I have a beautiful diamond necklace,
It sparkles when I wear it.
Keerthi Sriram, Kindergarten
Scholars Academy, CA

High Merit Poems – Grades K, 1, 2, and 3

Hockey
I play really hard,
I score a lot of goals.
To get the puck,
You need to play defense,
You can't let the other team score.
To play hockey,
You need to feel it, skate fast,
Score a lot, and pass.
Shaun Scott Rios, Grade 1
Scholars Academy, CA

Searched
S eals are calm animals.
E arly morning seals wake up.
A fter they wake up they eat.
R ed was on the seal's belly.
C alm seals won't hurt you.
H appy seals will always love you.
E very time you see a seal you will smile.
D id you see a seal today?
Aaliyah Benavidez, Grade 3
Midland Elementary School, CA

My Parents Are Important to Me
My parents are important to me.
My mom helps me do my homework.
My mom makes hot meals for us.
She takes care of us when we are sick.
My dad works hard to make money.
He buys us many things.
He pays for our education.
My parents are great!
Shaheer Imran, Grade 3
Islamic School of San Diego, CA

Soccer
I love soccer!
I kick the ball
I run to the ball
I kick the ball to the goal
I love soccer!
Sofia Abdalla, Grade 1
Horn Academy, TX

An Awesome Father
A father really honest and wise,
God gave him to me.
All I have is because of my father,
All that I can see.

A father with Athena's wisdom,
A father with Zeus's strength.
A father, clever and strong
Who goes the extra lengths.

A father who is really grand
A gentleman, I guarantee!
I always admire my father
And I know he loves me.
Alexander Nguyen, Grade 3
Montessori Learning Institute, TX

That's the Way I Like It
Roses are red,
Violets are blue,
And I love teachers, just like you!

School is fun,
We learn a ton,
And that's the way I like it!

I love the way you smile,
You make the leaves unpile,
Because you have your very own style.

And that's the way I like it!
Caleb Sims, Grade 3
John Hightower Elementary School, TX

Cooper
C all his name, he will come
O h so funny and sweet
O h so nice and furry
P et his back
E xtremely cute
R eady for some fun
Callie Hester, Grade 1
Horn Academy, TX

Shadows

Shadows
Walk
In the night
See them reflecting
The moon
Is that a bee?
Or a bear
Walking around
The street
I'm shaken with fear
But that is just shadows
They fool us all
Claire Claypool, Grade 3
Horn Academy, TX

Christmas

Giving presents
Getting presents
It is so fun!
Santa Claus
Jingle bells
Christmas songs
I just love it.
Christmas tree
Lights, ornaments
And all of the
Other stuff
Christmas!
Genevieve Grobler, Grade 1
Horn Academy, TX

My Kitten

My kitten is a black silky baby
When she gets in the sun
Her fur shines
One night
She was standing on my bed
I was reading a book
So I couldn't see her
She was right next to me!
I love my cat.
Lucy Feeney, Grade 1
Horn Academy, TX

Dreaming

When you sleep
you go into different
worlds —
worlds made out of
macaroni, magic, and metaphors.
Anything can happen
in dreams.
You could live in a castle or a cabin.
You could have
nightmares
happy dreams
sad dreams.
Anything can happen.
Peyton Robb, Grade 2
Gause Elementary School, WA

Rainforests

Rainforests are so interesting
with everything going on
Rainforests are so fascinating
With all the animals there
Ring-tailed-lemurs, butterflies,
Monkeys, elephants, leopards,
Red-eyed-tree frogs, toucans,
and parrots.
Rainforests are so intriguing
Don't you
think so?
I do.
Harlie K., Grade 3
Spring Creek Elementary School, WY

Spring

Spring, spring, spring is here.
It's a wonderful time of year.
The birds are here and sing a song.
And days to play get long.
The air is clear, you can play.
Play a game outside each day.
Spring, spring, spring is here!
It's a wonderful time of year.
Eric Soltanovich, Grade 1
Woodcrest School, CA

High Merit Poems – Grades K, 1, 2, and 3

Electricity
I love electricity.
I love how it travels through a wire.
It helps me use computer to check my grades.
It lights the city at night.
It generates water.
It connects everyone in the world.
Electricity is the best invention.

Izzah Kamran, Grade 3
Islamic School of San Diego, CA

My Dog
My dog, Amber likes to run up and down the house,
She sleeps at her doggie bed in the corner of my room at night.
She wakes me up in the morning like an alarm clock,
Then she goes downstairs and wakes up the three other dogs and five cats.
Then she goes back upstairs and pounces on all of the family.
My mom takes her on her walk,
she comes back and I go to school, I come home and it happens all over again.

Emmanuel George Sgouros, Grade 2
Annunciation Orthodox School, TX

The Mighty Vacuum
A young boy cleans his room with a new vacuum cleaner. As it sucks up dust, it grows as big as a bed. The boy lets go and falls on the floor. The vacuum is alive, sucking up everything in the house. Now it is as big as a giant monster. It rolls into the city and sucks up buildings. The boy says, "I'll stop it." He grabs a rope, he climbs up as if he's on an elephant, and once he reaches the top, he turns off the mighty vacuum! A feast was made for the boy. When he got home, he went to the bathroom to wash his hands. Bubbles shot out of the faucet.

Joseph Wyble-Ceno, Grade 2
Annunciation Orthodox School, TX

What Is Snow
What is snow?
Is snow icy white crystals that fall from the sky?
What is snow?
Is snow frosty frozen rain droplets?
What is snow?
Is snow tiny flaky cold pellets?
What is snow?

Zoe Chang, Grade 2
Annunciation Orthodox School, TX

Horses
Horses are brown, white, and gold.
Horses sound like trotting.
And smell like the countryside.
It wants me to ride it as fast as lightning.
Valentina Quintana-Sanchez, Grade 3
Wilchester Elementary School, TX

Earth
Colorful flowers
Nature animals crawl around
Earth is so awesome!
Jennifer Mackenzie, Grade 2
Horn Academy, TX

Asteroids
Very fast bam crash
Making holes in the moon
Space junk on fire
Moin Uddin Nomani, Grade 2
Horn Academy, TX

Butterfly
Flapping gentle wings
Bright colorful insect
Flies into the sky
Macy Fortenberry, Grade 2
Horn Academy, TX

Birds
Fly through the blue sky
Stop and sit on brown branches
Birds in the air fly
Kavi Shah, Grade 2
Horn Academy, TX

Little Brothers
Very tiny pests
Annoying little creatures
Making much trouble
Maggie Tran, Grade 3
Horn Academy, TX

Stars in the Sky
Stars in the sky,
Shining bright,
Searching everywhere.

Looking for friends,
To play with them,
Until the night time ends.

Stars in the sky,
Ready for bedtime,
Saying their goodnight prayers.

I'll see you tomorrow,
When the moon comes out,
And all the people are in bed.

Stars in the Sky.
Hannah Nors, Grade 3
Robinson Elementary School, TX

Spring
I see butterflies flying around.
I hope they don't touch the ground.

I see green leaves blowing past.
They are going so fast.

I see people go to the park.
They immediately leave when it's dark.

When I feel the warmer days.
I jump up and shout out yay!

I see grasshoppers jumping high.
They almost touch the sky.

I see people having fun.
They never want it to be done.
Vaughan Anoai, Grade 2
Woodcrest School, CA

Lollipops
Lollipops!
Shiny lollipops,
Sweet lollipops,
Grape lollipops,
Hard lollipops,
And sticky lollipops, too!
I love lollipops, how about you?
Sahily Interian, Kindergarten
A E Arnold Elementary School, CA

Lollipops
Lollipops!
Crunchy lollipops,
Sticky lollipops,
Red lollipops,
Juicy lollipops,
And hard lollipops, too!
I love lollipops, how about you?
Faith Lyons, Kindergarten
A E Arnold Elementary School, CA

Lollipops
Lollipops!
Small lollipops,
Red lollipops,
Hard lollipops,
Good lollipops,
And sour lollipops, too!
I love lollipops, how about you?
Mia Earley, Kindergarten
A E Arnold Elementary School, CA

Lollipops
Lollipops!
Golden lollipops,
Tasty lollipops,
Hard lollipops,
Round lollipops,
And soft lollipops, too!
I love lollipops, how about you?
Dean Onesti, Kindergarten
A E Arnold Elementary School, CA

Lollipops
Lollipops!
Sweet lollipops,
Hard lollipops,
Small lollipops,
Yummy lollipops,
And bumpy lollipops, too!
I love lollipops, how about you?
Logan Cashio, Kindergarten
A E Arnold Elementary School, CA

Lollipops
Lollipops!
Red lollipops,
Sour lollipops,
Hard lollipops,
Sweet lollipops,
And yummy lollipops, too!
I love lollipops, how about you?
Hailey Rios, Kindergarten
A E Arnold Elementary School, CA

Lollipops
Lollipops!
Blue lollipops,
Super yummy lollipops,
Blueberry lollipops,
Awesome lollipops,
And juicy lollipops, too!
I love lollipops, how about you?
Caleb Keeble, Kindergarten
A E Arnold Elementary School, CA

Lollipops
Lollipops!
Hard lollipops,
Yummy lollipops,
Slippery lollipops,
Small lollipops,
And circle lollipops, too!
I love lollipops, how about you?
Karissa Lomban, Kindergarten
A E Arnold Elementary School, CA

Strawberries

A juicy red fruit it is
It looks like it has chicken pox
It's so yummy
Even though it's in my tummy

They're the best when eaten in the summer
I love them
Even though they aren't sweet
They don't smell like stinky feet

I'm hungry for strawberry fizz
That is so fun to make
It tinkles my throat
But at least it doesn't taste like a coat

Strawberries they are
So sweet
I like to them for dessert
But I'm glad it's not as dry as a hot desert!

David Gao, Grade 3
Top Kids Center, CA

So Many Things

So many things from here to there,
So many things everywhere.
So many things I'll miss,
So many things I want to kiss.

So many things that I came to love,
Even the nature up above.
So don't forget me;
This was like my family.

When I came here I thought everything was bad,
But then I realized that I was glad.

So many things from city to town,
All these things I'll miss will make me feel down.
If you miss me just remember, I'll miss you.

Goodbye.

Henry Lemersal, Grade 1
Morning Creek Elementary School, CA

High Merit Poems – Grades K, 1, 2, and 3

Me
Aidyn
Fast, runs, walks
Loves P.E.
Who feels happy
Who needs kisses
Who gives kisses
Who fears nothing
Who would like to visit Texas
Caveness
Aidyn Caveness, Grade 1
Kentwood Elementary School, CA

Emily Is
Emily
Softball, loving, confident
Loves family a lot
Who feels happy
Who needs a blanket
Who gives love
Who fears war
Who would like to see Albuquerque
Hakanen
Emily Hakanen, Grade 1
Kentwood Elementary School, CA

Car Wash
Wash here, wash there.
Wash everywhere.
Get some soap, get some water.
It's a car wash!
Spray the car.
Get the soap and rub it on.
Get the water, spray it down.
It's a car wash!
Caroline Ashley, Grade 3
Wilchester Elementary School, TX

Trees
Trees are beautiful.
Trees have bark, bugs and beetles.
Trees are fun to climb.
Orrin French, Grade 3
Nenahnezad Community School, NM

Mary Grace
Sweet
Fun
Happy
Always there for me
Never mad at me
We play together
We sit together
We're always there together
Birthday parties
Sleepovers
Hangouts even too
We always are friends
She is such a good friend
Always there for me
Even Ashlyn too
Maddie Badger, Grade 3
Wilchester Elementary School, TX

Swimming
I like swimming
That is what I see
Swimming is all for me
So I learned that
Swimming is fun
So it is now my
Destiny
I had set
My goal
To become
A master
Try and try
I will
Never give up
Never in my life
Maximiliano Hernandez, Grade 2
Horn Academy, TX

The Doll
Dolls are cutie pies
I love very pretty dolls.
I love them the most.
Avery Terry, Grade 1
Highland Park School, MT

Shining Stars
Shining stars
High above the Rocky Mountains
Shining stars
Shine on the solid rocks
Shining stars
Shining against fire-lighted autumn trees
Shining stars
Shining over a flying eagle
Shining stars
Reflecting light from the ground
Shining stars
Catherine Dang, Grade 3
Annunciation Orthodox School, TX

I Hunt, I Hunt
I hunt, I hunt
a joyful sky.
I hunt, I hunt
strong men to help me on
my journey.
I hunt, I hunt
spirited animals such as flying
fish, dancing sheep, and a running cow.
I hunt, I hunt
a happy sun to lead me
on my journey.
Roberto Cortes, Grade 3
Annunciation Orthodox School, TX

All Around the World
First name Monnie
Is good, happy, funny
Love school, puppy, bunnies
Is good at sewing, math, games
Feels happy, lazy, sleeping
Wants toys, games, colors
Fears bad people, bad times, no fun
Likes to eat candy, chocolate, food
Watches Long King, God, Sanda
Is a resident of Ewa Beach, Hawaii
Last name Johnny
Monnie Johnny, Grade 3
Keone'ula Elementary School, HI

Flying
I am flying, flying, flying
Oh feel the wind blowing
Whoosh, whoosh, whoosh
It is so peaceful the wind is blowing
Whoosh, whoosh, whoosh
It is so peaceful.
The wind is blowing harder
Whoosh, whoosh
I am going higher and higher
Now I am so high
The houses seem like dollhouses
And people seem like dolls.
Finally the wind settles
Whoosh
And I land
Jennifer Schmalz, Grade 3
Horn Academy, TX

Rainbows
Rainbows are pretty big,
And colorful.
They come after storms,
Which is delightful.
God sends them down,
When,
The clouds move away—
Then we have fun,
For the rest of the day.
The sun will come
Out
And no rain will be falling.
Rainbows are fun,
Big,
And delightful.
Cylar Taylor, Grade 3
Valley View Christian School, MT

Birds
The birds are flying.
Babies hatching in the nest.
Hear the birds chirping.
Tobias Chow, Grade 1
Montessori Learning Institute, TX

Sharks and Minnows

Sharks
Fast, flaky
Eating, fighting, horrifying,
Teeth, mouth, fish, cyprinid
Hiding, moving, swimming
Small, cute,
Minnow

Sienna Tatro-Humphreys, Grade 3
McDowell Mountain Elementary School, AZ

The Colors of Life

If I were brown I'd be a bird, soaring through the sky!
If I were black, I'd be a clock, watching the kids doing their work in school.
If I were green, I'd be a jungle big and strong!
If I were yellow, I'd be the sun, shining so bright!
If I were white, I'd be a cloud, in children's sweet dreams…
If I were blue, I'd be the sky, so big and wide…
If I were red, I'd be a heart, pumping strong with all of the love that I have inside!

Callum Graham, Grade 3
Harloe Elementary School, CA

Skylanders

Are they animals or men
Pokemon and Skylander are not alike
They are both animal and man, they're a blend
A water jetback that shoots harpoons describes Gilgrunt
The lightning rod is my favorite feature
An awesome dragon, Spyro likes to shoots fire as he hunts
But Lightning Rod is my favorite creature!

Drake Mills, Grade 3
Jack Harmon School, AZ

Funky

Wow! That is a funky, silly clown.
It has fuzzy blue hair, red squishy nose,
and his big face is painted scary.

I am frightened scared, but the red clown
did have an awesome red and blue t-shirt.
The clown was a happy and funny crazy clown.

Arianna Gonzales, Grade 3
H W Schulze Elementary School, TX

All About Me

First name Airey
Is tired, playful, funny
Loves 3-D's, brother, mother
Is good at origami, sewing, games
Feels happy, playful, sad
Needs milk, brother, dad
Wants chocolate, lots of food, milk
Fears geckos, zombies, monsters
Likes to eat rice balls, salmon, sandwich
Watches *Tom and Jerry*, *SpongeBob*, *Power Rangers*
Is a resident of Ewa Beach, Hawaii
Last name Deer

Airey Deer, Grade 3
Keone'ula Elementary School, HI

Love

Kids love to play in the cold snow.
They think it's like a party with the midnight glow.
The sound of music sounds like the wind blows.

Laughing happy children playing,
listening to the Christmas music and singing carols.

Happy, mad, or sad today,
everybody loves this day.

Romantic days, romantic nights,
you choose what fits you just right.

Izaya Pena, Grade 3
H W Schulze Elementary School, TX

Chocolate

I am chocolate with a fancy pattern.
I live in a store inside of a yellow wrapper that looks gold.
My favorite colors are all colors. Color reminds me of being in the store.
Sometimes I like to ear white, but I usually wear plain brown.
My job is to make people happy when they're sad.
My family and friends are other types of chocolate.
I go on vacation in human bodies when they eat me.
My favorite holiday is being on sale, because then more people want to buy me.
I move when I'm in a person's pocket.

Tess Connerty, Grade 3
CLASS Academy, OR

High Merit Poems – Grades K, 1, 2, and 3

Peace

Love your neighbors, Jesus once said
Don't bear false witness, tell the truth instead
For all the gospels we learn each day
We must spread his word and always pray
Share the peace with your friends and family
Even with those who dislike you wholeheartedly
Go to church and reflect on His blessings
And do His will without second guessing
If you live each day with peace and love
You will certainly be rewarded from above

Sydney Sadiarin, Grade 3
St Joseph School, HI

Cat

My cute cat Spice loves to play.
Every time me and Spice play,
he's always so very funny.

Spice is a handsome white and sort of orange.
He's so fluffy, and soft at the same time.

Spice will always care and love you, no matter what.
Spice is just so loving, and caring to me.
I will never forget about my little baby Spice.

Alexandria Garcia, Grade 3
H W Schulze Elementary School, TX

My True Best Friend

My true best friend makes the sun come out.
She makes the birds sing.
She makes me laugh and she makes me shine.
My best friend makes me want to fly.
When I'm alone she comes and says,
"my true best friend you are in my life,
you make me shine so bright."
So will you come along and make the birds come out and sing?
Will you make me sing and fly?
Will you make the sun shine so bright?

Daytral Willie, Grade 3
Tatum Primary School, TX

Shark

Great White
Strong, dangerous
Swimming, eating, hunting
Fin, teeth, tanks, algae
Swimming, chasing, glowing
Small, tiny
Fish

Philip Huffman, Grade 3
Tracy Learning Center - Primary Charter School, CA

My Little Brother

I have a baby brother, his name is Jesse James.
He is special in his own way.
When he runs, laughs, and plays, he brings a smile to your face.
He's fast when you have a plate, he'll grab your food and run away.
He shows love in his own way.
He's the greatest baby brother I could ever have.
Remember, his name is Jesse James because he is the smartest of the gang.

Anthony Wheeler, Grade 3
Tatum Primary School, TX

Flowers

F orget-me-nots
L ilies
O rganic
W onderful
E nergy
R adiant
S mell ever so good

Ashlan Lucero, Grade 3
Tracy Learning Center - Primary Charter School, CA

Mostafa

R uns fast
A wesome
S illy.
H ilarious person.
E ats candy sometimes
E nergetic
D anyal's my friend

Mostafa Rasheed, Grade 3
Islamic School of Muslim Educational Trust, OR

High Merit Poems – Grades K, 1, 2, and 3

Rainbow
Red is a flower
Blue is the ocean
Yellow is light
Green is grass
Purple is love
Orange is the sunset
setting on the water
Camden Fox, Grade 1
CLASS Academy, OR

Frog
Tadpole
tiny, wiggle
growing, changing, hiding
eggs, pebbles, lily pad, bugs
leaping, swimming, sleeping
fast, poisonous
Frog
Caitlyn Gayrard, Grade 3
Ygnacio Valley Christian School, CA

Strawberries
A strawberry is sweet, juicy
and cold.
It looks round,
red, and also like a
heart. It feels
soft, chewy and
squishy.
Randal Begaye, Grade 2
Nenahnezad Community School, NM

Mom
Mom
Lovable, helpful
Shopping, hugging, kissing
High heels, lipstick, phones, trucks
Playing, working, hugging
Joyful, sweet
Dad
Alejandra Ramirez, Grade 3
St John's Episcopal Day School, TX

Brothers
Tim
Alike, boys
Fighting, playing, troublemakers
Twins that look alike
Jon
Timia Greenlee, Grade 1
Kentwood Elementary School, CA

Snake
Snake, scary, scaly, smooth and fast,
Snake, big, small, and long.
Snakes move at all different speeds
And there are all different kinds snakes.
All have a tail.
Leo Hsu, Grade 3
Jacob Wismer Elementary School, OR

Soccer
Me
Playing soccer
Saturday
Soccer field
Because I like it
Giovanni Tucker, Grade 3
Little Oaks School, CA

Crack
my house is cracking
what should I do?
My roof is falling my house
is cracking what should
I do!
Preston Chen, Kindergarten
All Seasons Children Learning Center, CA

Mountain Climbing
The frosty freeze on my cheeks.
The shiver going down my spine.
Marching in deep snow.
Hiking up and down mountains.
Ernie Reyes, Grade 2
Pleasanton Primary School, TX

Eagles Flight
See the eagle rise for flight
At the edge of a big cliff side
Spreading its wings far and wide
At the bright signal of the sun
Ready to fly for a long, long time
Kristin Xu, Grade 3
Horn Academy, TX

I Like the Park
I like the park!
I like the park!
I swing high
I swing low
I love the park!
Leore Nates, Grade 1
Horn Academy, TX

Dancing
Dancing
Point your toes
You will look pretty
Act like a ballerina
Make a big smile
Katherine Young, Grade 1
Horn Academy, TX

Aggies
Aggies Aggies score score score
Aggies Aggies we want more
Aggies Aggies hear the crowd roar
Aggies Aggies two, three, four
That is the scoreboard adding more
Alex Lasater, Grade 3
Wilchester Elementary School, TX

Longhorns
Horns, horns, horns fight!
We will never fail!
Baseball, football, swimming,
Track and field, lacrosse, and basketball.
Longhorns will never fail!
Cade Harger, Grade 3
Wilchester Elementary School, TX

X-ray
I hate when I get an x-ray.
They make my broken leg burn.
They bend it —
They make it like they're breaking it.
I hate it.
Keaton Klasing, Grade 3
Wilchester Elementary School, TX

Cheetah
hot, bad
rough, furry, hard
yellow, brown, black
growling, chomping, thumping
loud, hissing.
Yuta Haratsu, Grade 3
Wilchester Elementary School, TX

I Have a Name and It's Arman!
A is for awesome at work.
R is for really brave.
M is for mighty.
A is for amazing at basketball.
N is for nice.
Arman Arya, Grade 2
New Horizon School LA Campus, CA

Frogs
Frogs are green
Gooey
Mushy
Cool
They jump high!
Kade Richardson, Grade 1
Horn Academy, TX

My Tree
My tree is nice
The leaves brush in the wind
Apples fall off the leaves
Spring comes
Repeating
Caden Olbekson, Grade 2
Horn Academy, TX

High Merit Poems – Grades K, 1, 2, and 3

The Central Pacific Railroad
It's the 1800s
But the Central Pacific Railroad
Is beginning
At Promontory Point
The Central Pacific
And
The Union Pacific
To make
The Transcontinental Railroad
Kirby Gray, Grade 2
Horn Academy, TX

Beautiful Nature
Birds sing
Here and there
Pretty flowers everywhere
Green
Grass
On the field
Hopping here and there
What do you think is
There?
Nina Zhang, Grade 2
Horn Academy, TX

Ice Cream Sundae
Ice cream sundae
Why?
It is good
It has M&M's, whipped cream
and a cherry on top.
The best part is ice cream!
Morgan Wilson, Grade 1
Fir Grove Elementary School, OR

Rivers
Boats can float on rivers,
Rivers can make leaves float, too.
You can have a boat race in a river,
And you can row a boat in a river,
It's fun to swim in a river.
Cassandra Chan, Kindergarten
Scholars Academy, CA

In the Sea
The world is known to hold
The human race.
And in the world
Is one strange place.

If you thought
You were fast
To the waves you would be last.

The most amazing things
Are in the sea.
Not on land
With you and me.

Big or small
Short or tall.
The most wonderful things
Are here for all.
For all to see
In the sea.
Wylie Jones, Grade 2
Los Feliz Charter School for the Arts, CA

What a Dog Knows
What does a dog know?
It knows a perfect cat to chase,
family before friends,
petting,
sniffing,
fetching,
my food,
begging.
It also knows…
playing,
love,
scratching,
eating,
the table when we eat,
loyalty,
kindness and a
wet, slobbery kiss!
Abbie Samp, Grade 3
Spring Creek Elementary School, WY

Starfish/Whale

Starfish
Short, star
Floating, crawling, sticking
Tide pools, oceans, plankton, deep sea
Growing, eating, swimming
Scary, vicious
Killer Whale

Jonathan Hedrick, Grade 2
Tracy Learning Center - Primary Charter School, CA

Sun and Moon

Sun
Hot, bright
Burning, heating, warming
Star, ball, asteroid, holes
Gleaming, shining, illuminating
Rocky, hard
Moon

Sasha Lang, Grade 2
Tracy Learning Center - Primary Charter School, CA

A Weirder World Every Minute

Concrete turns into water,
Windows are the nets of fly swatters.
Trees lie around,
The roads are twisted every direction: left, right, up, and down.
Houses look like potters,

All because of an EARTHQUAKE.

Jaden Johnson, Grade 3
Hewitt Elementary School, TX

Angel and Devil

Angels
Beautiful, nice
Flying, playing, teaching
Halo, wings, horns, fire
Cackling, throwing, running
Ugly, mean
Devil

Lyda Nadery, Grade 3
Tracy Learning Center - Primary Charter School, CA

High Merit Poems – Grades K, 1, 2, and 3

The Color Red

Red is the color of kindness and care,
Red is a sweater that somebody wears,
Red is not lightning,
Red is a shock,
On Mars, red is a rock.

It's Rudolph's nose,
It's a pretty red rose,
Red is a heart that never goes far.
It's the beauty that calls your name,
It might be a parrot's feather,
Or a pretty red sunset from Mother Nature's weather.

Red is for pink,
Red is for purple,
Red is never for guzurple!

Red is a pretty color,
Red is not blue,
Red is for love!

Aubrey Alexander, Grade 3
Marguerite Hahn Elementary School, CA

Love

I got home from the bus, and saw a big dog.
It was so exciting.

I loved it so much, that I was very happy.
Then we went to the toy mall.
I got him a little hat.

He loved it so much,
and I bought him a little toy bed.

He loved it too.
He plays with them a lot,
until he gets sleepy.

He looks so cute when he is asleep,
then he wakes up and yawns.
It is a good day.

Abigail Tovar, Grade 3
H W Schulze Elementary School, TX

Ding Dong

Ding dong, it's midnight
Hear the boats' motors run
The morning has begun

Hear cars start to go
What a great dawn show
Look at the moon glow

The lights are bright
What a wonderful night
A new day is taking off.
Shade Brokaw, Grade 3
Rock River Elementary School, WY

Kaydon

I am smart and funny
I wonder what my mom is doing
I hear what people say.
I see everything around me
I want to go to college.
I am talkative and nice
I pretend that I'm in the Army.
I worry about my family
I dream about being a skater
I hope I pass third grade
I am happy and creative.
Kaydon McElroy, Grade 3
McCoy Avenue Elementary School, NM

The Dog

The dog
With black fur
And brown,
Loving, sweet Boxer,
Taken from dad, to coworker.
I miss him,
With loving heart,
Will always
Remember,
Gentle, baby dog
In San Francisco.
Kaylia Summerfield, Grade 2
Robert L Stevens Elementary School, CA

A Wild Forest

Full of wild creatures,
Flying birds, geese on the water.
Lakes shining, with flowers near,
Trees growing in peace.
Dark green leaves falling,
With butterflies fluttering around.
Frogs hopping, squirrels climbing,
A forest full of smells.
Aviva Bechky, Grade 3
Medina Elementary School, WA

Gorilla

Gorilla
Big as a tree
Punching
Walking
Wrestling
Banana hunting
Black
Grrrrrrr!
Alma Xotchitl Larios-Chacon, Grade 1
Johnson Elementary School, NV

The Zoo

When you go to the zoo,
What do you do?
If I go to the zoo,
I'll see some giraffes,
Or maybe have some laughs.
I might even see a tiger or two,
With my friend Lexi Lu.
Lexi Luna, Grade 3
Tatum Primary School, TX

Blue

Blue is the color of the sky.
Blue is a sound of a Blue Jay.
Blue is a feeling of water.
Blue is the smell of blueberries.
Blue is the taste of blueberry juice.
Blue is the sound of a waterfall.
Ashley Rawa, Grade 3
Hewitt Elementary School, TX

High Merit Poems – Grades K, 1, 2, and 3

Army

A is for Army, America's best
R is for reveille, the way they wake you up from rest
M is for military, they put you to the test
Y is for the yellow ribbon you wear on your chest

Liam Marchi, Grade 1
St Joseph Catholic School, CA

Labrador

Labrador, Labrador
Cute as can be.
He's so cute,
He hypnotized me.

Michayla Cain, Grade 3
McDowell Mountain Elementary School, AZ

Coconut

Brown small coconut
waits impatiently to drop
then plop,
it cracks open.

Danielle Greene, Grade 3
McDowell Mountain Elementary School, AZ

Seahorse

Seahorse, seahorse,
Swimming in the sea.
Orange pinkish,
Pretty to me.

Faith Shannon, Grade 3
McDowell Mountain Elementary School, AZ

The Toaster

My toast, it's alive! It really was a magic toaster,
I probably shouldn't have bought it from the guy
with the long beard, the pointy hat, and wand.
Oh yeah how could I forget the evil laugh? "Ahhhhh" my toast it's eating me ru-

William DuBois, Grade 3
South Bosque Elementary School, TX

About My Life
First name Joshua
Is funny, awesome, weird
Loves mom, bunny, dad
Is good at football, karate, Xbox
Feels good, active, mad
Needs food, clothes, supplies
Wants nerf gun, Legos, Hot Wheels
Fears scared, sad, work
Likes to eat Shumai, sushi, shrimp
Watches *Star Wars, Ben-lo, Spider-man*
Is a resident of Ewa Beach, Hawaii
Last name Keohohou
Joshua Keohohou, Grade 3
Keone'ula Elementary School, HI

Baylor Bears
B est college ever
A lways cool
Y ou rock
L et's go Baylor
O utstanding
R un, we don't want to miss the game

B e strong
E ven babies could beat the other team
A nd their playing
R ock on Baylor Bears
S core by Baylor Bears
Caroline Steen, Grade 3
South Bosque Elementary School, TX

Cheetahs
The
Cheetahs may
Seem cute, but they are
Very dangerous. If you make
Them mad, they will attack you.
If you leave
Them alone, they
Will leave you
Alone
David DeCamp, Grade 3
Horn Academy, TX

2nd Grade Best Friends
Breanna and Alyssa have
Two bangs
Four ears with earrings but only 2 pairs
Two pairs of pants
Two necklaces
Two bracelets
One short hair
One long one and
One great friendship.
Breanna, Grade 3
A E Arnold Elementary School, CA

The Life of the Wild
The life of the wild is a
red foot having to step
in a juicy fruit cactus.
It is a light yellow piece of
corn with streaks of magenta.
It is a colossal tent on fire in
front of rocky, lofty mountains.
The great wildlife enters the
world through the vivid sky.
Madison Phillips, Grade 3
Annunciation Orthodox School, TX

Rain
Rain, Rain,
Why do you always come down?
You're so loud,
And you boom
And you crash
And you bang!
Miles Fitzgerald, Kindergarten
The Presentation School, CA

Light
Light is really bright.
I see light at night.
I see light in sight.
The light can burn my eye.
The light makes me say goodbye.
Laura Mota, Grade 2
St Helen Catholic School, CA

High Merit Poems – Grades K, 1, 2, and 3

Pencil Sharpeners

Pencil sharpeners — 0 — pencil sharpeners
Why do you eat my pencils?
When I want to sharpen my pencil
I look at it and see it so sharp.
But then the second it touches my paper,
The tip of my pencil breaks in two!
Today it broke!
Yesterday it broke!
Big sharpeners!
Small sharpeners!
There are all types of pencil sharpeners in the world.
Everyone should be able to sharpen their pencils!

Ayden Samii, Grade 1
Woodcrest School, CA

A Happy Life

First name Jadelyn
Is nice, creative, funny
Love reading, swimming, school
Is good at sewing, origami, math
Feels happy, joyful, loved
Needs house, water, food
Wants shoes, big television, computer
Fears darkness, failing, tests
Likes to eat egg rolls, chicken nuggets, fried rice
Watches *Sponge Bob*, *iCarly*, *Victorious*
Is a resident of Ewa Beach, Hawaii
Last Name Nguyen

Jadelyn Nguyen, Grade 3
Keone'ula Elementary School, HI

My Dog Lefty

Lefty is like a fast horse,
His feet go so quick,
He likes to be free in the yard,
In the grass he makes a dirty trick.

His feet go like a fast guardian,
My dog sprints two times faster than my dad,
I try to chase him but he is too fast for me,
He is my papa's lad.

Hailey Mota, Grade 3
Oak Park Elementary School, CA

The Sea!

The sea has pinching crabs crawling on the ripe yellow
sand and big blue whales eating yummy fish. There are also
colorful seahorses dancing hip-hop in the water, and
sparkly waves splattering side to side. That is the sea!

Wade Arntzen, Grade 2
Annunciation Orthodox School, TX

Ride

R iding waves is hard.
I got used to riding the waves.
The **D** eal is stay balanced on the board.
E lephants can't ride waves on a surfboard.

Lucas Rubio, Grade 3
Midland Elementary School, CA

Poetry Book

P atty gave me a Nook.
O scar gave me a cookbook.
E than gave me a book that shook.
M e, all I want for Christmas is a poetry book!

Isabella Williams, Grade 3
John and Myrtle Hightower Elementary School, TX

Fall

Fresh, turkey
cold, windy, leaves
colorful, red, yellow, orange
laughing, singing, screaming, windy, buzzing

Mia Hallmark, Grade 3
Wilchester Elementary School, TX

snow

cold, fresh
hard, cool, round
falling, covering, snowman, snow angels
cracking, rubbing, laughs, giggles, chattering

Kyle Dessens, Grade 3
Wilchester Elementary School, TX

High Merit Poems – Grades K, 1, 2, and 3

my cat
witch hazel eyes.
lethal claws.
midnight nose.
little tiny toes.
she growls.
she pounces.
she scratches.
she purrs!
Aidan Bright, Grade 3
Whidbey Island Academy, WA

Rainbows
I love rainbows.
They are so beautiful.
Wonderful, beautiful rainbows—
Misty, beautifully made.
It makes me feel good inside,
When I see rainbows.
Wonderful,
Because God made all.
Caleb Pitcher, Grade 3
Valley View Christian School, MT

Playground
Kids running everywhere —
climbing like little monkeys.
Help me!
I think there are too many kids
going down slides
and
falling off the tornado.
It's a zoo out here.
Trenton Keeler, Grade 2
Gause Elementary School, WA

Cupcake
Cupcakes are sweet,
cupcakes are juicy,
cupcakes are good to eat,
now it is time for me to leave to school,
I'll find a hiding place just for you to cool,
when I go to school I'll think about you,
when I come back I'll eat you,
from my chin to my lip!
Sophia Echeverria, Grade 3
Meadows Elementary School, CA

Leprechaun Angels
Soft wings,
up in the air,
Hiding behind clouds,
tricky to catch,
But I can try.
There are pots full of gold,
I'm going to get it,
I found one!
Junior Hernandez, Grade 2
Robert L Stevens Elementary School, CA

Christmas
There are cookies
We get to eat
Candy canes
We get gifts
From Santa Claus
We celebrate Hanukkah
And Christmas
Too!
Aaron Byun, Grade 1
Horn Academy, TX

My Pet
My pet is a hamster,
he plays with his bouncy soccer ball,
and he eats lots of carrots.
His home is a green and blue cage.
I love my pet because he is so fluffy!
Steve Rios, Grade 2
Mesa Vista Elementary School, TX

Cats
Cats are cute
Cats are playful
You can play
With them
All day
Jade Paz, Grade 1
Horn Academy, TX

Page 43

My Creature

My creature is big and scaly
It breathes fire
It can also fly and dive
I can go outside and take a ride

It looks scary but it really is not
My creature is nice
But it doesn't look like it
It's not human being

It lives in caves but they're not seen
My creature is a fantasy
It is used in fairy tales
But it's usually evil

If you don't know what my creature is
You'll find out as soon as I finish
Don't be scared
But it is a dragon

Katherine Ye, Grade 3
Top Kids Center, CA

Seeds of Kindness

Plant seeds of kindness,
To grow a kindness tree.
That will drop kindness flowers,
All over you and me.

One way to be kind,
Is to share with your friends.
Kindness is forever,
Kindness never ends.

Compliment others,
That's what you do.
If you want to have a friend,
Be one too.

There are many ways to be kind,
Many ways, you see.
If we all work together,
We can plant a kindness tree.

Savannah List, Grade 2
Arroyo Vista Charter School, CA

Spring Time

Green leaves are growing.
Butterflies are showing.

In the garden I see ants.
I see gophers in the plants.

I see the squirrels climbing trees.
I also see insects, like bees.

I see the grass growing.
I see many people mowing.

I see the breeze through the trees.
Some people have allergies.

I see lots of seeds sprouting.
I don't see children pouting.

Chloe Silver, Grade 3
Woodcrest School, CA

Spring Has Sprung

Spring is now really here
And summer isn't very near

Birds are flying into trees
They eat bugs and yummy fleas

Sunny days are going by
Birds are flying very high

Rain is coming down in showers
It helps water a lot of flowers

Planting trees is a lot of fun
It takes weeks to be done

I plant a lot of seeds
Where there are no weeds

Vicky Wang, Grade 3
Woodcrest School, CA

I Am Rain

I am rain.
I can live anywhere but I like visiting Mount Hood.
My favorite colors are sky blue and snowy white
Because they are the colors I turn.
I like to wear clothes of water and mist.
My job is to water the planet.
My family is rain and my friends are clouds.
I go on vacation to Water Works.
My favorite holiday is Groundhog's Day
Because I like to give the groundhog a shower before he comes out.
I move with the water cycle.

Nicolas LeWarne, Grade 3
CLASS Academy, OR

The Sugar Crystals

Weightless crystals
Fast and fluffy cotton balls
Miniature flower petals are soft and shimmery
Lovely dancing snowflakes fall in the woods
Dissolving sugar crystals fleeing away
Puffy snowflakes are very watery
Snow as silky as a ribbon
I like to see the snow falling down
It is fun to play in, and it's fun to throw snowballs
Making a snowman out of circles
Can you please not throw snowballs at me?

Tipanga Storms, Grade 3
Lolo Elementary School, MT

The Loving Wind

I see the flowers,
I say they are pretty.
The flowers say it back to me.

The clouds are angels,
slowly floating up in the sky.
I think of butterflies picking me up
and flying me around and then back to my home.

The grass is warm on my face,
The flowers are warm too.

Genevieve Paul, Kindergarten
Mosaic Academy Charter School, NM

Summer
In the summer, I love to play all day,
We go to the beach and stay by the bay.

We have fun when we play ball in the pool,
And that helps us stay cool!

There I saw many fish,
The next thing I knew, they were on my DISH!

On the beach the kids make lots of castles,
I saw that building them is a big hassle!

After playing in the sun all day, I become hungry,
If the food takes too long, I get very angry!

When I finish eating, I like to have candy,
That's why I try to keep it handy!

Very soon it is time for me to go to bed,
I am not tired, but that is what mom said.

This is what my summer is like,
When I don't go to the beach, I will ride my bike!
Mariana Kamel, Grade 3
St John's Episcopal Day School, TX

Nature
The gleaming stars shooting
across the shimmering sky.
In Amarillo, the tough
bull dashes through
the Duro Canyon.
Peaceful people grow soft cotton.
Sheep are herded across the
smooth plains.
Big tepees are glazed like cake icing across
the gorgeous land.
Paw prints are left like birth marks in the soil.
Fragrant flowers bloom in the humid spring.
Thousand of beautiful birds sing and soar across the
cloudy sky.
Tess Boukouzis, Grade 3
Annunciation Orthodox School, TX

High Merit Poems – Grades K, 1, 2, and 3

Everything
There are noses
and roses.
Fun math
Or a bath?
Fun dogs
and snorty hogs.
There are fishes
and wishes.
Yogurt
and tube-like Go-Gurt.
There are big cups
and cuddly pups.
Stores
Or S'mores?
There are streams,
hopes, and dreams.
There are books
or new-styled nooks.
There's a dog mix
which is a good pick.

Daniella Arevalo, Grade 3
St Anthony Immaculate Conception School, CA

Excited
Playing soccer, hiding out, running fast
and trying to find gold treasure.
They all get excited.

Going to the wonderful park,
watching eagles soar across the sky.
I love them all.

I'm sure a lot of people love them too.
Some people might feel like singing loudly,
or dancing fast.
Some people might feel that it's boring.

Playing fun games, watching television,
searching for fun things,
a lot of stuff gets me excited.
What about you?

Armando Rocha, Grade 3
H W Schulze Elementary School, TX

Bumble Bee
Oh pretty little bumble bee
Flying over me.
Way up high in a tree
Way down low on my knee.
Ouch you stung me!
Crazy little bumble bee
Buzzing all around me.
Demi Johnston, Grade 1
Meadows Elementary School, CA

Walking Through the Stars
They sparkle all around me,
Through that inky veil of dark,
Sparkling brightly through the night,
As I look,
I feel so special,
Like a sparkle,
In the night.
Lily Hughes, Grade 3
Edward Byrom Elementary School, OR

About Me
The important thing about me
is that I'm nice.
It is true that I was a baby
I am a child, and I am a student.
It is true that I want to be a doctor.
But the important thing about me
is that I am nice.
Alondra Ontiveros, Grade 2
Vista Square Elementary School, CA

Feather
F eathers are light,
E very feather is bright,
A t any place there's a feather in sight,
T here's a feather to your right,
H ere's a feather at night,
E very time you squish it it gets tight,
R each a feather in its soaring flight.
America Flores, Grade 3
Edward Byrom Elementary School, OR

Sun/Moon
Sun
Bright yellow
Gleaming, sparkling, shining
Sunglasses, sweaty, dark, cold
Circling, cooling, ending
Gray craters
Moon
Ella Classen, Grade 3
Horn Academy, TX

Hand/Foot
Hand
Big, small
Reaching, throwing, writing
Hand clean, foot stink
Walking, running, skipping
Stinky, smelly
Feet
Matt Munn, Grade 3
Horn Academy, TX

Waterfall
Waterfall
Peaceful water
Flowing, soaring, gleaming
Down to the riverbank
Shining, flowing, gleaming
Wet water
River
Whitley Seborn, Grade 3
Horn Academy, TX

My Family
My family is nice.
They help me a lot.
They give me warm foods.
My mom makes my lunch every day.
They take me to school.
They buy me what I want.
I love my family.
Ilyas Syed, Kindergarten
Islamic School of San Diego, CA

High Merit Poems – Grades K, 1, 2, and 3

Rain Forest
Tropical rain forests are cold,
rainy,
peaceful,
happy,
tropical,
and full of animals.

Brandon Loo, Grade 3
McDowell Mountain Elementary School, AZ

Inside
I opened the garage and out came a car
I opened the car and out came a person
I opened the person and out came a brain
I opened the brain and out came a thought
I opened the thought and out came words
I opened the words and out came a poem

Chloe Lipitz, Grade 2
Seattle Jewish Community School, WA

I Am Special
The important thing about me is that I am special.
It is true that I was a baby and I grew.
It is true that I am a student.
It is true that I am 7 years old.
But the important thing about me is
that I am special.

Italia Neyoy, Grade 2
Vista Square Elementary School, CA

Snowy Owl
There once was an owl white and small.
Who lived on the ground with no sun at all.
In the night he would eat his prey.
But, in the morning, he would sleep all day.

Laken Wise, Grade 3
McDowell Mountain Elementary School, AZ

Raiders
They are a good team
They play in the NFL
They are my favorite

Armando Magana, Grade 3
Tracy Learning Center - Primary Charter School, CA

A Celebration of Poets – West Grades K-3 Spring 2012

Skiing
Skiing fast
Skiing slow
Skiing high
Skiing low
Skiing down
Skiing up
Skiing is fun
Emma Hickman, Grade 1
Horn Academy, TX

Sky
Big blue sky
High up above my head
So
Beautiful
with so many
White fluffy
Clouds
Zoila Lazo, Grade 3
Horn Academy, TX

Room and Bed
Room
Fun, exciting
Playing, laughing, thinking
I have fun in my room
Sleeping, dreaming, laying
Soft, warm
Bed
Jacob Lavorini, Grade 3
Horn Academy, TX

Robots
Engine
Eyes
Hands
Wheels
Mouth
Wire
Robots
Bruno-Nicolas Fittipaldi, Grade 1
Horn Academy, TX

Play
I like to play my DS
I like to play wrestle
I like to play Wii
I like to go to soccer
I like to go to Disney World
I like to go to Canada
I like to play it's fun
James Kimzey, Grade 1
Horn Academy, TX

My Bike
I love
To ride
My bike
I go for
Five or
Four laps
Around the block
Georgia Harris, Grade 2
Horn Academy, TX

Winter
Winter is cool!
When I go outside
My cheeks are as red as
Red can be
I love winter!
I love winter!
I love winter!
Quinn Hochglaube, Grade 1
Horn Academy, TX

Happy Birthday Dr. Seuss
Thing 1 and Thing 2 are the best,
The best of all! And so are you!
With their hair so blue,
They find lots of fun things to do!
We dressed like them on Halloween.
The party was great, we got crazy
Because we stayed up late!
Amanda Rubio, Grade 3
Hadley School, CA

High Merit Poems – Grades K, 1, 2, and 3

Book of Christmas
I like Christmas
Because Santa Claus
Gives presents
I like Santa Claus
Christmas
Is fun
Because We get
To put
Stuff up outside
Merry Christmas
Emily Serpas, Grade 1
Horn Academy, TX

My Mom
I hear her voice when
she is talking with my dad.
I want her kiss.
I'm happy when we play
I'm sad when she's not in the house.
I wish that she can live in
my house when I grow.
I believe that she will visit me
at my house.
I am her son.
Fernando Guerrero, Grade 2
Vista Square Elementary School, CA

Rattlesnakes
Rattlesnakes
Are bad
Snakes
When you
Steal their
Eggs you
Better give
Them back
Because they
Might attack!
Elijah Gurtzweiler, Grade 2
Horn Academy, TX

Shadows
Following me home
The mysterious figure
Silently creeps
Kate Hester, Grade 3
Horn Academy, TX

Fish
Fish are fun to watch
Aquarium fish are great
I love my clownfish!
Brock Lang, Grade 3
Four Peaks Elementary School, AZ

Winter
Playing in the snow
Sipping chocolate by the fire
On a cold, wet day
Hailey Heatherington, Grade 3
Four Peaks Elementary School, AZ

Water
Rushing wet water
Waterfall splashing liquid
Crashing down lower
Edward Chen, Grade 3
Horn Academy, TX

Flying Flowers
Buzzing bees flow by
Wind comes by and the tree blows
Flowers come like snow.
Oren Judy, Grade 1
Fir Grove Elementary School, OR

Zebras — A Haiku
With stripes black and white
And it lives in Africa
Swift horse of grasslands
Robert Weatherby, Grade 1
Weatherby Home School, TX

Pink Tulip
Soft as silk
A pink cloud in the blue sky
The floating smell of perfume in my nose
Cotton candy or a pink ball of fluff
Flapping angel wings all around in the silent woods

Rhett Matthew, Grade 3
Lolo Elementary School, MT

Belle
Belle
White, brown
Sleeping, begging, eating
Mom's little, special princess
Princess

Hunter Reed, Grade 3
McDowell Mountain Elementary School, AZ

Tear Drop
Tear Drop
Lazy, funny
Walking, eating, sleeping
She likes to sleep
Dog

Cody Cloud, Grade 3
McDowell Mountain Elementary School, AZ

Bluey
Bluey
Blue, playful
Swimming, staying, floating
Crazy for fish food
Fish

Gavin Duxbury, Grade 3
McDowell Mountain Elementary School, AZ

Yummy Yummy Cookies
Cookies
Sweet, delicious
Crunching, munching in my mouth
Peaceful, lovely treat
Goodies

Sydney Hatch, Grade 3
Tracy Learning Center - Primary Charter School, CA

Spring

S inging birds
P lants that are beautiful
R ain that makes plants grow
I like the beautiful smell of flowers
N uts from chipmunks
G ardens

Angelina Frediani, Grade 3
Tracy Learning Center - Primary Charter School, CA

Clowns

C an't stop goofing off
L oves to juggle
O ver again he honks his nose
W ears funky clothes
N ever forgets how to walk on a ball
S uper funny

Jason Piazza, Grade 3
Tracy Learning Center - Primary Charter School, CA

Football

Football is so fun. When you are done with your football game,
you can go to the San Antonio Park and play there all day.

You are so, so happy that in your chest,
your heartbeat is getting faster and faster.
You're having so much fun that you forget about football.

Salvador Martinez, Grade 3
H W Schulze Elementary School, TX

Green

Green is for the strong hulk and the fresh grass outside, too.
Green is for St. Patty's Day and green is for a four leaf clover.
Green is for half of the earth and green is for a cold, wet forest.
Green is my favorite color!

Elijah Shaw, Grade 2
Robert L Stevens Elementary School, CA

India

Has a lot of gold
Capital is New Delhi
My dad was born there

Sukhmani Dhadiala, Grade 2
Tracy Learning Center - Primary Charter School, CA

Sea

Oh sea,
crashing sea,
why don't you come to me,
with fingers of white on the tips of your waves?
I've welcomed you with open arms,
but yet you run away.
I hear that you are blue,
but you are clear.
I hear rumors of killer sharks that live in you.
You are not dangerous,
yet you seem so
because of your threatening waves.
Your only cause to threaten
is the dangerous animals and fish that live in you.
Your beaches shine in the sun like tiny gems.
You are so beautiful, sea.

Rhys Sharpe, Grade 2
Glacier View Christian School, MT

Moon

Moon
White, cold
Shining, reflecting, freezing
Night, rocks, fire, light
Burning, firing, exploding
Yellow, hot
Sun

Colton Dingman, Grade 3
Tracy Learning Center - Primary Charter School, CA

Christmas Is in the Air

You can smell it when the snickerdoodle cookies are
baking in the hot oven.
You can taste it when the cinnamon bread slips off my fork and
melts in my mouth.
You can hear it when the gold bells jingle, the horses gallop as they pull the
sleighs, and the children carol.
You can see it when the mistletoe is right above you, wreaths on every door,
and the happy looking snowmen are in the park.
You can feel it when the chilly wind blows on your face, the fluffy snow
touches your skin, and in the love from your family.

Vinutha Sandadi, Grade 3
A E Arnold Elementary School, CA

Teachers

The only thing teachers want to do is homework,
Oh, those teachers, will they ever be out of work?

Sometimes they are bossy, but oh so nice,
They have such good advice!

Every day they make my brain stronger,
Sometimes I wish the school day would be longer.

I'm grateful for everything they do,
That's why they love kids through and through.

Sabrina Ramirez, Grade 3
St John's Episcopal Day School, TX

Christmas Is in the Air

You can smell it when
the brownie is on the big plate.
You can taste it when the hot cocoa with small marshmallows
and cold whipped cream
goes into your mouth.
You can hear it when the people
are ripping their presents.
You can see it when
the lights go on.
You can feel it when the happiness makes you warm.

Joyce Koo, Grade 3
A E Arnold Elementary School, CA

Nature

When you step outside your door, there's so much to explore.
The grass is green.
The flowers blossom.
The wind blows.
The air is moist.
The birds are singing.
The bees are buzzing with honey.
The rain is pouring.
The leaves are changing colors.
Nature is a beautiful sight in all seasons.

Maryam Siddiqui, Grade 3
Islamic School of San Diego, CA

Elated

E arly in the day as sun rose.
L ong in the day, the seals might get hungry.
A s the waves went, the seal went too.
T hey sit outside and watch the waves.
E xploring is my favorite thing to do.
D eep in the water, it is so deep.

Lawrence Lee, Grade 3
Midland Elementary School, CA

Black Holes

Black holes will suck you up like a vacuum.
Black holes will stretch you like spaghetti.
Black holes shoot gamma rays that chastise you with their power.
Black holes are collapsed stars.
Black holes shift gravity into a twirling motion like a sad merry-go-round.
Beware…Beware…Beware!!!

Christian Smith, Grade 3
Saigling Elementary School, TX

Genice

G enice is my mom.
E mpathy she has.
N ice she is.
I deas she has also.
C unning she is.
E- mails she likes to check.

Gelina Schumann, Grade 3
Goethe International Charter School, CA

Math

Math is fun.
There's so much to learn.
You have division, addition, subtraction and multiplication.
But my most favorite learning happens during summer vacation.

John Chesney, Grade 3
Sunset Elementary School, WA

Brothers

Always there for you
They like to think about you
Love you very much

Harleen Dhillon, Grade 2
Tracy Learning Center - Primary Charter School, CA

Family

My family is super sweet.
They are the kind of people you want to meet.

We love to sing Christmas songs.
They are not too long,
So do not be scared to sing along.

We also like to Samba dance,
While the fun night lasts.

Naydean Santoya, Grade 3
H W Schulze Elementary School, TX

Grand Dad

G randson watched the seals.
R ocks are very hard.
A s Ben searched, he noticed a seal moving.
N ewly born seals need lots of love.
D o you like seals as much as I do?

D iving with the seals would be so neat.
A seal needs a lot of fish to eat.
D o you think seals are nice?

Alex Soto, Grade 3
Midland Elementary School, CA

Imagination

Rodolfo is like a non-stop, hard working machine.
A bear is like a fluffy rabbit.
Spaghetti is like a jump rope.
A marshmallow is like a soft cloud.
A pancake is like a big trampoline.
And Mrs. Chung is like a non-stop exerciser.

Rodolfo Chavez, Grade 3
Elder Creek Elementary School, CA

The Plains

A shiny stream runs through rocky plains,
and cold air comes to a blue sky at 11:45 at night.
A bull is running in fear and a 17 year old girl
   is humming while riding her fast horse.
Four girls and a horse are walking through the colorful plains.

Mia Katherine Stankowski, Grade 3
Annunciation Orthodox School, TX

Hurray for Spring
Flowers are sprouting out of the grounds.
Baby animals are making different sounds.

Warm weather fills the air.
Bugs are going everywhere.

Birds are flying to the sky.
They are flying way up high.

There are more sunny days.
The sun shoots out its rays.

Rain showers are coming down.
They are coming to every town.

Birds are going tweet tweet.
They are letting their chicks eat.

Animals are coming out of their hole.
Even a little tiny mole.

Seeds are sprouting along the way.
The animals are busy catching their prey.
Violet Josephson, Grade 3
Woodcrest School, CA

The Spooky Halloween Night
Halloween is finally here,
My favorite night just arrived.

I will be the brave knight,
Defending the ones who want to survive.

Be careful and don't make a mistake,
You might step on a scary snake.

A black cat is outside my house,
Waiting to attach a tiny mouse.

I am going to take a nap,
Now that I am awake, I hope to get a bat in my trap!
Santi Zermeno, Grade 3
St John's Episcopal Day School, TX

Seal Spring

S un shines on the seals.
P up rests in the water with her mom.
R ocky beaches are where the seals lay.
I n the water the seals catch fish.
N ext spring the seal surfed with the boy.
G rey seals swim in the cold water.

S he had three baby seals.
E ach day she had to catch fish for the three seals.
A storm hit and the baby seal got hurt.
L arge waves hit the shore.
S eal shines with her mother's love.

Cody Tucker, Grade 3
Midland Elementary School, CA

Soccer

Soccer is my favorite sport.
When I first started,
I was very nervous.

I started on a beautiful bright Christmas Day.
Soccer was very hard, but I got the hang of it.

My family always came to my soccer games.
The soccer field was very long,
as I was running.

My mom loved the beautiful sunshine in the sky.

David Garcia, Grade 3
H W Schulze Elementary School, TX

Party on Main Street

There's a party on Main Street,
Pedal a bike with your feet,
Down to the party on Main Street.
There are games; there are prizes,
And guess what? They come in all sizes!
Come on, it'll be fun! Life can't always be hard,
So relax, drop your guard.
You deserve a treat,
So come to the party down on Main Street.

Evan Finnegan, Grade 3
Edward Byrom Elementary School, OR

Roman's Life

First name Roman
Is funny, loving, lazy
Love dogs, iTouch, family
Is good at running, gaming, army building
Feels happy, sad, shy
Needs food, water, clothes
Wants crossbow, bow arrow, unlimited money
Fears dark, ghosts, drowning
Likes to eat shrimp, ramen, chicken
Watches Adventure Time, Sky-line, Mad
Is a resident of Ewa Beach, Hawaii
Last name Minear

Roman Minear, Grade 3
Keone'ula Elementary School, HI

All About Me

First name Makyla
Is picky, smart, hungry
Love family, bunnies, parades
Is good at crafts, feeding my dog, drawing
Feels happy, confident, shy
Needs trees, school, food
Wants dolls, money, ice cream
Fears bears, dying, ghosts
Likes to eat rice, Vienna sausage, chicken
Watches *So Random*, *Wizards of Waverly Place*, *Good Luck Charlie*
Is a resident of Ewa Beach, Hawaii
Last name Cortez

Makyla Cortez, Grade 3
Keone'ula Elementary School, HI

The Enthusiastic Eraser

I am an eraser.
I live in an awesome school called CLASS Academy.
My favorite color is green because it is the color of grass.
I like to wear pink pearls.
My job is to erase dirty pencil marks.
My family is three more erasers and my friends are pencils.
I go into binders for vacation.
My favorite holiday is summer break because I get to relax.
I move when people use me.

Aseem Agarwal, Grade 3
CLASS Academy, OR

High Merit Poems – Grades K, 1, 2, and 3

The Hit
I hope I hit this.
Could it be done?
It felt like it was in slow motion
but to everyone else it was in fast motion.
SLAM!
I knew it could be done. Going, going, gone...

Nathan Siciliano, Grade 3
Wilchester Elementary School, TX

Green
Green is a hummingbird as it flies through the sky.
Green is the sound of a frog croaking.
Green is the feeling of a turtle's shell.
Green is the smell of peppermint.
Green is the taste of mint ice cream.
Green is the color that is bright and beautiful.

Maggie Thaller, Grade 3
South Bosque Elementary School, TX

Autumn Time
A utumn is cool.
U mbrellas help to keep us dry.
T he summer days faded, now it's autumn.
U nder water seals swim.
M usic sounds cool.
N ight time is when sea animals sleep.

Lilia Carrasco, Grade 3
Midland Elementary School, CA

Marshmallows
Marshmallows... are so fluffy and soft like tiny pillows,
From the grocery bag to the pantry to your mouth,
Many flavors to choose from,
They are like airy clouds from food Heaven!

Karis Williams, Grade 2
Annunciation Orthodox School, TX

Friends
Friends, Friends, I have lots of them.
I've got mice, goats, bears, and of course humans.
Friends mean a lot to me, especially my best friends.

Avery Rump, Grade 3
Edward Byrom Elementary School, OR

What Is Green?

Green is the color of a country breeze
Washing my face like a shower place.
It stands for peace in my country of course,
And the color of the country's sights;
The movement of the turtle in the city pond;
The smell of the green lily pad in our state;
The sound of the frogs chatting around.
That is what's green I'm telling you now.

Brian Chen, Grade 1
Lincoln Elementary School, CA

Seal Pup

S eal pups are nice.
E verybody should love seal pups.
A seal pup is so tiny, they need a lot of help.
L oving them is not hard to do, since they're just so cute.

P eople should help save them.
U nless we start saving them, they will all start to slowly disappear.
P ups are really good swimmers.

Rommel Dunbar, Grade 3
Midland Elementary School, CA

Happy

The snow is falling out of the sky.
The bells are ringing very high.

The entertainment of the children playing.
The children love the loud bells ringing every day.

Most importantly there is happiness,
In the cold winter air.

Miranda Saiz, Grade 3
H W Schulze Elementary School, TX

Nature

Nature
Magical life
Loving, living, blooming
Living with beautiful light
Green

Elanah Brooks, Grade 3
Tracy Learning Center - Primary Charter School, CA

High Merit Poems – Grades K, 1, 2, and 3

Flying

Flying is very cool.
It is very exciting.

You can fly with the cute bird.
You can see them in the beautiful sky.

You feel the soft breeze in your face.
And feel the soft breeze pick up my brown hair.

And your clothes wave in the air.
You see the tiny little cute home.

You see the tiny little people,
and the beautiful butterflies,
their colorful wings.

Jose Escobedo, Grade 3
H W Schulze Elementary School, TX

Tiger

I was at the South Diego Zoo.
I saw a big tiger, and the tiger roared at me.

All I felt was a breeze.
My black hair flew back.
Then the other three little tigers woke up.

There standing in front of me were four big, and small tigers.
One tiger looked like the biggest king.

Then the other one looked sad.
The other two looked creepy and lonely.

Then I had to leave for my birthday,
so I said to them, "Bye!"

Deandra Velasquez, Grade 3
H W Schulze Elementary School, TX

Ocean

So green, white, and blue,
You can go boating on it.
You can swim in it.

Carrie Weiss, Grade 2
Tracy Learning Center - Primary Charter School, CA

Math Test
M an I wished I studied for my math test.
A w I'm really angry!
T esting is super hard,
H ard, hard. Am I

T errific or terrible?
E asy, it's not. It's
S o hard.
T esting is hard!
Kayden Clawson, Grade 3
Spring Valley Elementary School, TX

Blondie
Blondie eats the pellets,
Happily walking on the food.
She looks very greedy
Like a hungry cow dude.

Getting scared from my hand
That chick runs fast as the flash.
The tempo of her feet like a rock band
I can feel her lethal dash.
Joseph Agha, Grade 3
Oak Park Elementary School, CA

Spring
S ometimes it rains.
P opsicles are yummy in the sun.
R un and play in the yard.
I n shorts and T-shirts.
N othing better than spring.
G oing to the park to have a good time.
Sidney Dering, Grade 3
Edward Byrom Elementary School, OR

Monkey
There was a monkey named Banana
He lived in a forest in Montana
He has a long tail
He usually visits his friend, Whale
He never goes to the Savannah
Krishna Saxena, Grade 3
CLASS Academy, OR

River Oh River
River oh river, how blue
You are, the boats are in, drifting
In your current.

River oh river, how I love
The sun, gleaming on your
Waters. Your twists and turns I admire.

River oh river, the best you
Are, reflecting the sun's rays. How
Sweet your waters are.

River oh river, how respectful to
The people around. River, you will be
Remembered.
Kagan Sims, Grade 3
Rock River Elementary School, WY

Rain
The rain goes splish splash
It falls to the ground
The cold winter has begun
Splish splash
It hits leaves and roofs
Falls into lakes
Hits streams
Pitter patter
Drinking hot cocoa
Eating warm toast
Slurping tea
Splish splosh
Playing games
Snuggling in bed
Warm, happy
Beck Walthers, Grade 2
Laurence School, CA

Anaconda
The anaconda,
he squeezes his prey slowly,
he loves to attack.
Maximiliano Rodriguez, Grade 2
Mesa Vista Elementary School, TX

High Merit Poems – Grades K, 1, 2, and 3

Hunter

First name Hunter
Is smart, good at sports, creative
Loves school, video games, Pokemon
Is good at baseball, soccer, drawing
Feels happy, athletic, confident
Needs money, water, food
Wants Xbox, DSi XL, Yu-gi-oh
Fears clowns, dying, sharks
Likes to eat pizza, popcorn, candy
Watches *Clash of the Titans*, *300*, *Wrath of the Titans*
Is a resident Ewa Beach, Hawaii
Last name Hancock

Hunter Hancock, Grade 3
Keone'ula Elementary School, HI

Months

January, January how cold you are
February, February love flows in the air
March, March leprechauns jump in the grass
April, April rain falls to the ground
May, May flowers bloom everywhere
June, June summer is here
July, July my birthday is finally here
August, August it is so hot outside
September, September school starts again
October, October Halloween is here
November, November we are so thankful
December, December it is the end of the year

Regina Lee, Grade 1
Woodcrest School, CA

Treasures

Treasures, Treasures
Things that remind you of,
Trips and exciting things,
　　I wonder if I am going to get
A ruby or a gem,
A pirate's chest filled with gold!!!
Treasures, Treasures, COME TO ME!
Treasures are not just gold,
Treasures are trinkets that I hold dear in my little hands.

Maya Emerson, Grade 3
Edward Byrom Elementary School, OR

Danyal

D anyal is a good friend.
A fast runner.
N ice to people.
Y ou are great.
A lot of friends.
L ong time at MET.

Danyal Almakky, Grade 3
Islamic School of Muslim Educational Trust, OR

My Mom

My mom is super nice and beautiful.
She buys us everything we need.
She purchases interesting toys for us.
She helps me with homework and reading.
She cooks for us every day.
She is the best mom on Earth.

Sara Farah, Grade 3
Islamic School of San Diego, CA

Knowledge

Knowledge helps me in school.
Knowledge helps me write essays and poems.
Knowledge is what makes me a scientist and a math magician.
Knowledge makes me smart.
Knowledge helps me answer logically.
Knowledge is not just for me, it is for all.

Nafees Ahmad, Grade 3
Islamic School of San Diego, CA

Bald Eagles

Bald eagles eat fish, they swoop, they dive.
They eat their prey, like fish, alive.
You can see them on Arizona's mountains.
And flying above our famous fountain.

Parker Sweet, Grade 3
McDowell Mountain Elementary School, AZ

Lemonade

Lemonade Lemonade drip drop on a hot summer day.
Do you want some do you want some.
Then come on down today okay?

Britain Brooksby, Grade 3
Edward Byrom Elementary School, OR

High Merit Poems – Grades K, 1, 2, and 3

Cars
Cars go fast
Cars go slow
Cars are red
Cars are green
Cars are pink
Cars are purple
Jake Haegner, Grade 1
Horn Academy, TX

Music
The birds playing their beautiful music.
Together they bring the beautiful sounds.

They fly up into the sky, and they find
Their nest, then sing a lullaby.
In the morning the baby birds chirp.
Roman Ramirez, Grade 3
H W Schulze Elementary School, TX

Rainbow
Red is an apple
Blue is water
Yellow is the sun
Green is for Christmas
Purple is February
Orange is a pumpkin
Nikhil Nayak, Kindergarten
CLASS Academy, OR

Winter
I see snow
I hear Christmas carols
I taste hot cocoa
I feel cold
I smell cookies
I know the season is Winter
Olivia Mersereau, Grade 1
CLASS Academy, OR

Rainbow
Red is the color of CLASS Academy
Blue is the water
Yellow is corn on the cob
Green is sour grapes
Purple is a bow in my hair
Orange is a Thanksgiving color
Jaidyn Richter, Kindergarten
CLASS Academy, OR

Rainbow
Red is hot lava
Blue is Cookie Monster
Yellow is bright
Green is Oscar the Grouch
Purple is a Valentine color
Orange is the sunset
Richelor Pierznik, Grade 1
CLASS Academy, OR

God
God is the one
who brought me to life.
I'm thankful for that.
I am.
Isabel Stribling, Grade 1
Fir Grove Elementary School, OR

I Am a Busy Bee
I am a busy bee
What fun I can be
I get all my honey for free
I am a busy bee!
Brenna Powell, Grade 3
The Brook Hill School, TX

Butterfly
Peacefully it soars
So gracefully fluttering
As it drinks nectar
Ava Cruse, Grade 3
Horn Academy, TX

Sea Animals
Seashells are hard
Sea turtles can swim and walk
Waves splash like milk
Oceana Jin, Grade 2
Horn Academy, TX

Shadow

Tiptoe, tiptoe,
here comes the shadow
in the night.
Tiptoe, tiptoe,
thump, thump, thump, thump!
Getting louder and louder.
Tiptoe, tiptoe,
the shadow getting closer and closer,
click…
I turned on the light,
oops, that was my day!

Hikaru Tashiro, Grade 3
Jacob Wismer Elementary School, OR

All About Me

My name is Kelechi,
And I am five,
I like to swim,
But do not dive.
I have two eyes,
They are bright.
I see the sun during the day,
I see the moon at night.
My hands are soft,
My hands are small,
I like to play with them and throw a ball.

Kelechi Ajawara, Grade 1
Scholars Academy, CA

Kids

Naughty kids
Nice kids
Helpful kids
Loving kids
Any kind of kid will do
Smart kids
Fearless kids
Blind kids
Energetic kids
Any kind of kid will do
I'm just glad to have you

McKinzie Rasmussen, Grade 3
Urie Elementary School, WY

Heartbeat

I love heartbeats.
I think it means happy.

When you run,
it's your heart beating fast.

When you are happy,
your heart beats slow,
sometimes not all the time.

It is fun to have a happy heart beat.

Ariel Villanueva, Grade 3
H W Schulze Elementary School, TX

Spring

Spring! Spring! Spring is here!
It's an awesome time of year.
I see birds flying here.
And animals come out to be found.
Birds are here with a sweet sound.
The warm weather makes me so proud.
And I love the animal clouds.
It's nice to look around.
I see bugs crawling on the ground.
Spring! Spring! Spring is here!
It's an awesome time of year.

David Lenchitsky, Grade 1
Woodcrest School, CA

Sun

Sun, sun, sun
You shine
Light
Every day
But your beautiful
Light
Gives light
To the plants
Every day
I just want to say
We need you

Genesis Moreno, Grade 2
Horn Academy, TX

High Merit Poems – Grades K, 1, 2, and 3

Purple Is…
Purple is a vase,
Like the makeup on my face,
Purple is like ink,
Its best friend is pink!

Purple can be time,
Like when it's a quarter to nine,
Purple can be very soft,
Like everything that I saw in the loft.

Purple can be paint,
I might even faint!
The color looks so nice,
It's as cool as ice.
Jyla Roberts, Grade 3
Marguerite Hahn Elementary School, CA

A Loyal Friend
A pet is very loyal,
some of them can dig in the soil.
Others can fly,
They soar above the trees and into the sky.

Some can swim,
A fish is a pet that has a fin.
You can have a reptile, too,
The amazing things pets can do!

You can find one here, or there,
I am sure you are a pair.
Pets are loyal friends,
And I am so sad that this is the end.
Alice Davine, Grade 3
John Hightower Elementary School, TX

Fire
Fire
Orange, hot
Moving, burning, spreading
It doesn't feel cold
Painful
Jeremiah Yonemura, Grade 3
Ygnacio Valley Christian School, CA

Tea Party
Once I had a tea party,
I invited all my friends,
I decorated my room,
And got my best tea set out,
I served them tea, cookies, cupcakes,
And fruit rolls too.
We all sang party songs,
It was fun,
We had lots to do.
Ranjani Raveendranath, Kindergarten
Scholars Academy, CA

In the Rainforest
The rainforest is big and
a little bit dark,
they don't have dogs
like we see in the park.

The bugs are small,
we like them all,
when you see them prance,
you'll want to dance.
Muriel Mora, Grade 3
Goethe International Charter School, CA

Frisco
He eats the mail faster
Than you can say jumping
Jacks on Jupiter. He is
Fast. He does not like
Swimming. All he does is
Sleep. He is afraid of big dogs.
Miles Sachdeva, Grade 2
Annunciation Orthodox School, TX

Rainbows
Rainbows are really colorful.
Sometimes they come when it's sunny.
People see them better when it's cloudy.
Rainbows are seen every day,
High above in the Milky Way.
Mirna Flores, Grade 2
St Helen Catholic School, CA

Rocky Mountain

Rocky Mountain
Down in the Rock Mountain
Rock Mountain
Children laugh and play on the dark green grass
Rocky Mountain
Young men are dancing around the fire, talking to the spirits
Rocky Mountain
Women making buffalo meat for everyone
Rocky Mountain
Everyone runs over to eat
Rocky Mountain
All the people go back into their leather tents
Now you can only hear the cry of the coyote
Rocky Mountain

Arielle Herrera, Grade 3
Annunciation Orthodox School, TX

My Un-favorite Season

Now autumn's gone and went so slow
But in comes winter with pounds of snow
Another season would be fine
But as for winter I would not pay one dime
I'd beg, I'd plead to anyone
But still right now I see no sun
Any why you ask I don't like this season
Well I can tell you more than one reason
Now first I say it is no fun
'Cause I can't play without a sun
And second I don't like the snow
How hard the winter breeze does blow
And now you get it's not my favorite
But still I might just want to save it

Ellie Conway, Grade 2
St Joseph Catholic School, CA

Snowflakes

Snowflakes are white.
Snowflakes have different shapes.
Snowflakes are small.
Snowflakes are big.
No one can stop the snowflakes from falling.

Alondra Armenta, Grade 2
Mound Valley School, NV

High Merit Poems – Grades K, 1, 2, and 3

Grandma
Pretty, gentle
Helping, cleaning, baking
She is very nice to everyone.
Grandmother
Kayleigh Cadman, Grade 3
Nenahnezad Community School, NM

Uncle
Tall, funny
Laughing, eating, loving
Picks on us
Relative
Rachelle Teswood, Grade 3
Nenahnezad Community School, NM

Dad
Tall, smart
Working, bigger, eating
My dad loves hanging out with me
Father
Cheyenne Benally, Grade 3
Nenahnezad Community School, NM

Dog
Bushy, furry
Running, licking, jumping
Protects you everywhere you go.
Friend.
Dominic Cambridge, Grade 3
Nenahnezad Community School, NM

Pitbull
Cute, fun
Protecting, chasing, loving
I play with them when I can.
Strong
Kierra Jones, Grade 3
Nenahnezad Community School, NM

Tiger
Strong, big
Roaring, eating, running
Tigers never give up.
Baby cub
Vydazia Mariano, Grade 3
Nenahnezad Community School, NM

Igloo
Cold, small
Dwelling, freezing, building
We have to wear a heavy coat.
Home
Rakeem Begay, Grade 3
Nenahnezad Community School, NM

Popcorn
Buttery, sweet.
Warm, soft, slick.
Yummy, yellow, crunchy, delicious.
Crunch, pop, chomp, smack, crackle.
Drew Arend, Grade 3
Wilchester Elementary School, TX

Rabbit
White, small
Hopping, jumping, eating
Eats carrots and cabbage.
Bunny
Keienna King, Grade 3
Nenahnezad Community School, NM

Sharks
The shark eats fish,
The shark has a family,
Sharks have very pointy teeth,
The shark loves to be in the water.
David Olivas, Grade 2
Mesa Vista Elementary School, TX

Rain

Raindrops dropping on the leaves
The sky is gray
No birds flying
Puddles splash as people walk
So windy outside
The rain falls to the ground
Making big puddles on the floor
Drip drop, splash goes the rain
It makes sounds when I'm inside
When it is bedtime I can't go to sleep
Because the raindrops will not stop dropping

Mysteri Gebbia, Grade 2
Laurence School, CA

The Mystery Me!

I'm fun!
I dance!
I love to sing!
I sing in the tub all of the time.
I sing no matter what.
My favorite singers are Beyonce and Nikki Minaj.
Nobody can tell me not to sing.
I was born with it.
I need to use my gift.
I like rap and hip hop.
What do I want to be when I grow up?

Ajah Henderson, Grade 3
Tatum Primary School, TX

Spring Time

S pring time is fun because seals come.
P laying with seals would be so much fun.
R eport if you see a hurt seal.
I 'm going to help seals when I grow up.
N o seals were hurt in this story.
G ray seals are so very cute.

T hinking about seals is a lot of fun.
I would save a seal if it was hurt.
M eet a seal because there so cute.
E arth needs more people to help the seals live a long time.

Jalan Hall, Grade 3
Midland Elementary School, CA

Rainbows!

Beautiful red, green and blue
There are 7 colors it is true
The rest are orange, violet, yellow
And also the color indigo
When the rain is falling,
And sun comes out shining,
When the fog clears,
A rainbow appears
At the end of a rainbow there's a pot of gold
Shining, glimmering, standing out bold

Sanjita Rishikesan, Grade 3
Medina Elementary School, WA

Peace

Peace is looking up at a rainbow in the sky
With colors of joy in the blue sky
The rainbow spreads out as you look at it
When you see the sky
You look back at the rainbow,
It slowly disappears
When it fully disappears
You can only see the clouds
And the blue, blue sky
That is peace

Alison Shaw, Grade 1
Laurence School, CA

Enjoying the Stars

The sky was dark, but the stars lit it.
It was now colorful, with an aurora in the sky.
Two eagles soared in the evening sky, close together, but falling down.
White mountains, a deer stood on top, mighty and strong.
In a forest, it was dark, but finally I reached home, with fireflies lighting the sky.
At the beach, colorful seashells, making the sand blue and pink.
Little fish swimming around, different colors, blue, black, pink, red and brown.
I turned around, I heard coyotes howling, I felt a soft breeze, I laid down on the grass,
ENJOYING THE STARS!

Ramya Reddy, Grade 3
Jacob Wismer Elementary School, OR

A Celebration of Poets – West Grades K-3 Spring 2012

Cherry Trees
Cherry tree looks nice
A cherry tree is nice looking
it looks pretty also.
Shilo Burson, Grade 1
Fir Grove Elementary School, OR

Feather
Gracefully flowing
Down so silky strings as it
Lands so quietly
Sophia Swanston, Grade 3
Horn Academy, TX

Rain
I don't like
the rain on me.
I can't go outside and play.
Hailey Masterfield, Grade 1
Fir Grove Elementary School, OR

Fire
Fire, it is so hot
See the flames fly, it's so bright
Ashes.
Brooklyn May, Grade 1
Fir Grove Elementary School, OR

My Mom
I love my mom so much.
She is nice.
I can't stop thinking about her.
Karla Santiago-Mendez, Grade 1
Fir Grove Elementary School, OR

Tiger
Big scary tiger
Running through the jungle
Looking for some food
Nikolas Statiras, Grade 3
Horn Academy, TX

The Puppy Has Gone Crazy
The puppy has gone crazy!!
What should we do,
He's gone in my house
Doing crazy things.
Happy to see me,
We try to give him food.
Then he stops,
He goes to sleep like an angel,
In a cozy basket.
Messy house, but finally quiet.
Neomi Gonzalez, Grade 2
Robert L Stevens Elementary School, CA

The Ladybug
As I look in the grass,
I see something red and black,
like a little ball hiding.
As tiny as a pea.
As red as a rose.
As black as the night.
I grabbed it,
then it flew away
into the white, poofy clouds,
that looked like snow.
Dalila Hernandez, Grade 2
Robert L Stevens Elementary School, CA

Spring Is Here
Hello flowers
Hello sun
Now what to do
It's time to run
Goodbye snow
Goodbye ice
Goodbye rainwater
It's too nice!

Hello beautiful world!
Edee Polyakovsky, Grade 2
Seattle Jewish Community School, WA

High Merit Poems – Grades K, 1, 2, and 3

Spring Time
Birds are flying around in spring.
The mama birds will always sing.

In spring we have more sunny days.
In spring honey is what bees praise.

You can celebrate Easter in spring.
In an egg you just might find a ring.

In spring you can plant seeds.
A plant is what a gopher needs.

In spring there will be rain showers.
The showers will really help the flowers.

The flowers are very very pretty.
You don't really see them in the city.

The animals are just waking up.
You just might see a new born pup.

Spring to me is the best.
It's so good I just can't rest.
Jalen Short, Grade 3
Woodcrest School, CA

Piece of Wood
Piece of wood
You were
Cut down.

Piece of wood
You fell to the
Frozen ground.

Piece of wood
You were found.

Piece of wood
I see you
Right now.
Ella Endres, Grade 2
Seattle Jewish Community School, WA

My Old House
The house was amazing!
The house had lots of fun stuff.
I wish I could still be there.
I loved my old house so much.
I lived close to my very best friend,
But now I don't. I loved my room.
I had so many toys.
My attic had a big art section.
I miss my old house so much!
Abigail Goldenberg, Grade 2
Horn Academy, TX

Eyes
I look
into the
distance
and I'm
aware of
the
beautiful
world around
me
Shai Tratt, Grade 2
Seattle Jewish Community School, WA

Green
Green is the sound of the birds that sing,
Green is the color of a sparkling ring,
Green is the color of the way that's up,
Green is the color of a water filled cup,
Green is the color of everywhere,
Green is the color of a big, bold stare...
Savannah Johnson, Grade 3
Speegleville Elementary School, TX

Dragon
There once was a dragon named Fire
He was never a liar
He likes mice
But not in his rice
He liked to play dice with mice and a tire
Aditya Sood, Grade 2
CLASS Academy, OR

Page 75

I Am a Book

I am a book.
I live in a public library.
My favorite color is white because it is the color of my pages.
I like to wear jackets that keep me warm and safe.
My job is to entertain people.
My family is the librarian and my friend is the bookshelf.
I go on vacation to the book fair.
I like it because people will buy me and take me home.
My favorite holiday is the book sale.
I move when people turn my pages.

Rohan Shetty, Grade 3
CLASS Academy, OR

Happy

Happiness is cool. Happiness can be loved.
When I am happy I throw a marvelous party.

And all my cool friends come over to my nice house.
We sing into the pink microphone.

Sometimes we have popcorn sleepovers at my house.
I go to the Kingsborough Pool, and I see my cool friends
splash each other in their pretty faces.
We color and draw heart pictures.

Madalynn Orosco, Grade 3
H W Schulze Elementary School, TX

My School

I love my school,
It is big and clean,
It is where I meet my friends,
It is where I learn to read and write,
It is where my skill in numbers has grown,
And so has my curiosity in a lot of things.
Learning at school is a lot of fun,
With teachers so smart and patient to teach me,
And tell me to be a smart kid,
Which I am too!

Hannah Arellano, Kindergarten
Scholars Academy, CA

Sydney

S is for my name, Sydney.
Y is for one of my favorite colors, yellow.
D is for my middle name, Davey
N is for my name!
E is for eating my favorite foods
Y is for my name spelled backwards, Yendys.

Sydney Wolfe, Grade 1
Broderick Montessori School, CA

Clock

I am a clock.
I live in a dull house, but on a colorful wall.
My favorite colors are black and white.
I like white because it is the color of my tummy.
And I like black because it is the color of my gears.
I like to wear gears because they change time.

Diya Lonial, Grade 3
CLASS Academy, OR

The Four Corners of Nature

The four corners of nature make me feel calm.
The four corners of nature sound like birds chirping, rushing waters,
    and feet stomping.
The four corners of nature look like fast waterfalls flowing straight down.
The four corners of nature smell like pine trees.
The four corners of nature are in fact the world.

Kate Phillips, Grade 3
Annunciation Orthodox School, TX

Snow

S eals love the water.
N ow it is daytime and time to play.
O n the shore it's warm.
W e went to see the seals at the beach that day.

Vincent Banda, Grade 3
Midland Elementary School, CA

Waterfall

Sparkling waterfall
It is very beautiful
I love watching it

Zoey Lipps, Grade 3
McDowell Mountain Elementary School, AZ

Purple

Purple is faith,
purple is the sunset on a calm coast.
Purple is a warm blanket,
or an enchanted fairy tale castle.
And purple is a fresh out of the oven cookie.

Amanda Whitehead, Grade 3
Speegleville Elementary School, TX

Football

Football is a fun sport.
You can throw it and run the football
And you can pass it and it is brown.
It is made from pigskin and it is the best sport ever
And it is fun.

Nigel Outley, Grade 2
Annunciation Orthodox School, TX

Seal Place

S eals love to swim.
U nderwater a seal will go to find something.
R ocks are where seals rest.
F ish don't like to get eaten.

Kylie Toomes, Grade 3
Midland Elementary School, CA

A Cat in a Hat

There once was a cat in a hat.
He chased a very big bat.
When its time for a nap.
He slept in a gap.
But he never gave up on that bat.

Muhammad Faks, Grade 3
Islamic School of Muslim Educational Trust, OR

Peacocks

Peacocks
Beautiful, colorful
Puffing out feathers to look good
Peacocks make me feel beautiful
Birds

Emma Brown, Grade 3
Tracy Learning Center - Primary Charter School, CA

Thankful

I am thankful for all my hands can hold —
A paintbrush that I can doodle with,
My dad's hand when I am scared,
And my fluffy cat.

I am thankful for all my eyes can see —
the colorful sunset that sets on the horizon,
Words that are written in a book,
And the brown butterflies that flutter by.

I am thankful for all my ears can hear —
Jazz that's from the trumpet,
The crash of the ocean waves,
And the snap of Rice Crispy treats.

I am thankful for all my mouth can taste —
The salt of white crab meat,
Tasty porridge that slides on my tongue,
Bubble gum that's juice tastes sweet.

I am thankful for all my nose can smell —
The scent of cupcakes flowing from the kitchen,
A turkey that smells spectacular,
And flowers blooming.

Corey Anesi, Grade 3
A E Arnold Elementary School, CA

Tyrus' Life

First name Tyrus
Is funny, lazy, creative
Loves sports, family, dogs
Is good a football, baseball, games
Feels happy, loved, tired
Needs family, water, money
Wants DSI, phone, iPad
Fears cats, family, ghosts
Likes to eat pizza, pie, banana
Watches I'm Number 4, Ghosts, Dogs and Cats
Is a resident of Ewa Beach, Hawaii
Last name Stephens

Tyrus Stephens, Grade 3
Keone'ula Elementary School, HI

Love

Love is   in the air
you can't   see   it but
it is   there
in the   air forever
  everywhere   in the
     air   everywhere
  everywhere   in the
            world.
Kiana Anderson, Grade 3
McCoy Avenue Elementary School, NM

The Important Thing About Me
The important thing about me
is that I am kind.
It is true that I was small
and I grew.
It is true that I am a student.
It is true I will be a baker.
But the important thing about me
is that I'm kind.
Samantha Rueda, Grade 2
Vista Square Elementary School, CA

Birthday Party
Birthday, awesome,
Can't wait,
Bouncy house,
Turning 8,
Presents, Legos and sweet treats,
Many people come,
Then the fun,
Love my birthday!
Vicente Mandeville-Martinez, Grade 2
Robert L Stevens Elementary School, CA

Kayden/Bubba
Kayden
obnoxious, picky
fishing, biking, reading
hardworking, student, kid
Bubba
Kayden Dibble, Grade 3
McCoy Avenue Elementary School, NM

The Pool
Down to the pool I went
I put my bathing suit on
I rush down to the pool
Dad throws me in
I went SPLASH
Got sister wet
Sister says don't get me
Wet again
Mikayla Scholz, Grade 2
Horn Academy, TX

My Friend
G abi is my short name.
A bby is my friend.
B lair is my friend too.
R abbits are my favorite animal.
I have another friend.
E lla, she is so nice.
L augh, Ella makes me laugh.
A guilar is my last name.
Gabriela Aguilar, Grade 2
Horn Academy, TX

The Wind
The wind
   whistles
through trees
   and bullets
through bushes.
It is going somewhere new.
But where is it going?
I wonder.
Ryan Tuite, Grade 2
Gause Elementary School, WA

Swampy/Frog
Swampy
Slimy, fun
Leaping, griping
Bug eater, line leaper
Frog
Hanna Brenner, Grade 2
Valley View Christian School, MT

High Merit Poems – Grades K, 1, 2, and 3

Books

Books are fun to read
They are interesting
They are spectacular
And funny
The pictures tell
What the words are telling me
Paragraphs,
Paragraphs, and paragraphs
So many words, and words
Mysteries and comics
Authors, publishers, artists
Dull colors,
Or no colors at all
Or dazzling and bright
Even imagination like
Fairies, dinosaurs, zombies,
Mummies, dragons,
And miserable
And horrifying giants
These creatures
Can be terrible, fun, or funny.
Zoe Chen, Grade 3
Horn Academy, TX

The Snowman

The snowman
Is soft, very soft
Wow!
The snowman
Is running
He has a
Snowball
He throws it like a ball
It went as fast
As a bullet
The snowman
Melted in the sun
We had a
Good time with him
I say goodbye
Snowman
Brandon Pham, Grade 3
Horn Academy, TX

Christmas

On Christmas Eve on a cold Sunday,
presents are delivered from happy Santa.

But not all kids get presents.
Santa knows if you're naughty,
like when you throw stuff inside.
You will get coal.

So be good kids because you probably
want presents, like Legos and dolls under
the fancy Christmas tree.
Madellyn Maldonado, Grade 3
H W Schulze Elementary School, TX

LEGO®

LEGO®s are fun and cool,
The things you build rule!

You can use them to create and build,
They will make you so thrilled!

Some people think LEGO®s are not fun,
I never want my project to be done!

You can build LEGO®s again and again,
They will always be your friend!
Marcelo Fernandez, Grade 3
St John's Episcopal Day School, TX

I Say Hello to Nature

I say hello to the wind
The wind says hello back
I like your gentle breeze
The wind says, "Thank you"
You're welcome
Hello, grass
I like how green you are
"Thank you"
You're welcome
A dragonfly lands on my arm
It is so peaceful
Gabrielle Aeschlimann, Grade 1
Mosaic Academy Charter School, NM

The Four Corners of the Plain
Run to a peaceful camp where a warm, crackling fire burns.
To a calm, peaceful lake where slimy fish swim.
To a hot, sandy island where a wiggly, scaly snake lives.
To a bad, hard war that goes on and on.
To a place where a soft, loud bird and a wise old woman live.
Be nice.
Be friendly.
For you are the grandmother of the plains.

Maggie McCarthy, Grade 3
Annunciation Orthodox School, TX

Hawks
Hawks, hawks here and there,
I see them everywhere.
On ranches and small farms,
They do not have any arms!
Their wings will take them anywhere,
Up and down though the air.
Don't try to destroy them, they don't want to end,
They're just trying to be our friend!

Mark Austin Wilkins, Grade 3
St John's Episcopal Day School, TX

Candy
Candy! Candy! How I love it! Candy! Candy! It's
so tasty! Candy! Candy! What would I do
without it? I love all types of candy!
Gobstoppers, Sourbelts, Half 'n Half, Laffy
Taffy, Reese's, Gum, and Crunch! But my
favorite is M&Ms! Oh, they're delicious,
scrumptious, truly amazing! Man, I'm hungry!
What would I do without it?

Danny Miner, Grade 2
Annunciation Orthodox School, TX

Red
Red is the sound of dynamite and the roar of the wild.
It's the excitement of a brand new book and the movement of a brand new car.
Red is the happiness of family and the power of victory.
It's as smooth as a bird's feathers, but it's as fierce as a tiger.
Red is the sound of the wind and the howl of the midnight coyotes.

Ed Brown, Grade 3
Speegleville Elementary School, TX

High Merit Poems – Grades K, 1, 2, and 3

Baseball
Baseball is fun
Hitting,
Catching,
Scoring runs,
Winning,
Losing,
Awesome!
I love baseball!
Samuel Efron, Grade 1
Horn Academy, TX

Heroes
Heroes are here to save the day,
They will try to save us in some way!
Their mighty powers are big and strong,
They will never do anything wrong.
Look at that, they are super tall!
Both of them got into a crazy brawl,
With their big arms, they take a WHAMM!
Then the villain goes away in a scram.
Derek Gomez, Grade 3
St John's Episcopal Day School, TX

Feather
Sometimes,
a feather floats by you
And you notice
its beauty and elegance
Maybe you see
a soft and fluffy wisp of down
And
you get into a trance.
Isabella E. Acosta, Grade 3
California Virtual Academies (CAVA), CA

Thanksgiving
I like Thanksgiving
I saw a turkey
And ate some apples
I like eating
Thanksgiving is fun!
Jalen Wright, Grade 1
Horn Academy, TX

Jonathan
Jonathan
Funny, fast, scared
Loves a lot of toys
Who feels happy
Who wants more race cars
Who gives presents
Who is afraid of roller coasters
Who would like to see a cheetah
Anderson
Jonathan Anderson, Grade 1
Kentwood Elementary School, CA

Myself
Karris
Fun, nice, smiley
Love parents a lot
Who feels pretty
Who wants a phone
Who gives love
Who is afraid of snakes
Who would like to see a pony
Wellington
Karris Wellington, Grade 1
Kentwood Elementary School, CA

Lubnaa
L is for lovely.
U is for unique.
B is for beauty.
N is for noble.
A is for artistic.
A is for awesome.
Lubnaa Abdul-Alim, Grade 2
New Horizon School LA Campus, CA

Family
Family
Sweet, kind
Loving, hoping, praying
Always there for you
Sweet
ShayLynn Voss, Grade 3
Rock River Elementary School, WY

A Celebration of Poets – West Grades K-3 Spring 2012

Best Friends
She is…
Crazy, silly, happy,
Awesome, nice, weird.

She looks like…
Strawberry blonde hair.
Hazel eyes.
Freckles.
Short
Turtle earrings.
Despina

She is…
Nice, kind, funny,
Cool, quiet, amazing

She looks like…
Black hair
Brown eyes
No freckles
Tiny
Diamond earrings
Cha-Cha

Best Friends!
Despina Quintana-Sanchez and Cha-Cha Stinson, Grade 3
Wilchester Elementary School, TX

Basketball
I like playing basketball
I play with my friends
At lunch we split into teams
Our team is Patrick, Michael, and Javier
And the other team is Anthony, Rocko, and Willfrado
We jump ball, they gets it, shoots it,
They make it, we check the ball
We pass, we shoot
We miss, we get the rebound
We make it, the crowd goes crazy
We win, the score is 17-9
I love to play basketball
Michael Ortega-Portillo, Grade 3
St Anthony Immaculate Conception School, CA

Feels Like Home

Every sound I hear
Tapping in my ear,
I feel the grass on my hands and toes,
The beauty of nature sweetly shows.
I see the breaking waves and hear them, too,
It's beautiful, beautiful I tell you.
The trees and the bushes,
The leaves and the berries;
Everywhere I look
There are little colored fairies.
The smell of bread
Is swirling inside my head,
In this green Paradise I roam.
It is here that feels like home.

Olivia Randle, Grade 3
College Gate Elementary School, AK

Spring

Butterflies are flying everywhere.
Maybe someday one will land in my hair.

Animals wake up from hibernation.
To count them all I use multiplication.

Animals with tiny paws won't break plants.
It is so hot maybe you won't wear pants.

There are earthworms crawling in the dirt.
Even if they're dirty that won't hurt.

Outside, there are many trees.
They sway because of the breeze.

Jocelyn Shek, Grade 2
Woodcrest School, CA

Pink

There was a girl named Pink
She really loved to play with ink
She loves her nanny,
And she has a friend named Panny!
When she drops a penny she likes the sound that goes clink.

Evelyn Jerde, Grade 2
CLASS Academy, OR

Lollipops

Lollipops!
Good lollipops,
Golden lollipops,
Sweet lollipops,
Roly lollipops,
And hard lollipops, too!
I love lollipops, how about you?
Aaron Nam, Kindergarten
A E Arnold Elementary School, CA

Venus

Voyaging volcanic Venus
A day on Venus is longer than your year.
Volcanic Venus — sizzling…cracking.
Clouds of sulfuric acid swirl overhead.
Reflecting Earth's motion…
When the sun sets or before it rises.
You, too, can see me.
Kyle Youngquist, Grade 3
Saigling Elementary School, TX

Gravity

Gravity is not fair,
It never lets you jump high into the air,
It's just completely unfair!
Even if your weight is light,
Gravity always puts up a fight!
And why are birds able to fly that high?
Gravity shouldn't let them fly in the sky!
Samuel Goddard, Grade 3
Wilchester Elementary School, TX

Rock

Rock
Big, round
Rolling, boring, rocking
Boulders, pebbles, stone, rock
Bobbing, rocking, rolling
Big, hard
Boulder
David Saether, Grade 3
Horn Academy, TX

The Beach

The waves whooshing taking me back
Playing with a bucket
Of sand
Going to make sandcastles
On the other side
SPLASH
The water comes to eat my sandcastle
Kaila Nayvelt, Grade 2
Horn Academy, TX

Feeding

Birds
Pretty, colorful
Cheeping, flapping, chirping
Birds eat little worms
Wiggling, slithering, jiggling
Slimy, icky
Worms
Nawar Ahmed, Grade 3
Horn Academy, TX

Foxes and Wolves

Foxes
Smart, stealthy
Stealing, hiding, spying
Four legged, smart dogs
Howling, hunting, spreading
Sly, fast
Wolves
Sernry Zhu, Grade 3
Horn Academy, TX

Meow! Bark!

Cats and fat cats
So cute and fluffy
Bull dog, gray hounds
And watch dogs go crazy!
Chinchillas, fish, and toads, too
What do I do to keep track of this zoo?
Meow! Bark!
Matthew Stuckey, Grade 3
Abercrombie Academy, TX

Mrs. Claus

Mrs. Claus, she helps her husband get ready for Christmas,
so do the tiny elves.

They are singers and helpers at the same time.
At night, Christmas Eve, all of Santa's brown reindeer
fly to every house to deliver lots of big toys.

I wonder how it looks in the colorful factory, where
the small elves make small and big toys.

Jazelle Sotello, Grade 3
H W Schulze Elementary School, TX

Spring

Spring! Spring! Spring is here!
It's a shiny time of year.
In spring we grow flowers everywhere.
And we see birds flying in the air.
And we always share fun.
And we always can see the sun.
We can open our windows to see the spring.
And we can seen an angel's wing.
I love spring!!!

Sarah Sverdlov, Grade 1
Woodcrest School, CA

Mice

Mice flee for cheese after the cat's rage
Mice take nibble by nibble till everything is devoured
After the people fall into a deep slumber
The mice will scamper at midnight
Mice are very puny compared to a cat's dreadful talons
And now you see how mice react.

Helena Tsigos, Grade 3
Annunciation Orthodox School, TX

Rain Water

Rain
Slippery, wet
Striking, dripping, splashing
Splashing gets you wet
Water

Annaliese Anaya-Morford, Grade 2
Tracy Learning Center - Primary Charter School, CA

Brother

My brother is very very funny.
He steps outside and it is sunny.
He grew up in Oregon like everyone else.
He makes funny jokes like an elf.
And he likes us all and himself.

Sarah Bashir, Grade 3
Islamic School of Muslim Educational Trust, OR

Fractions

The important thing about a fraction is that it is part of a whole.
It is true that the whole was cut into equal pieces.
You can eat a fraction of a pizza.
It can be small like 1/100 or it can be huge like 1/2.
But the important thing about a fraction is that it is part of a whole.

Gaynell Lopez, Grade 2
Vista Square Elementary School, CA

A Plant

The important thing about a plant is that it is green.
It is true that they need water, sun, and soil.
You can plant it in the ground.
It could be small or big.
But the important thing about a plant is that it is green.

Marco Zamora, Grade 2
Vista Square Elementary School, CA

There's Nothing Better Than Friendship

Friendship
Precious, awesome
Brightens gloomy moments
Rainbows treasure trove discovered
Always

Kamal Deas, Grade 2
Tracy Learning Center - Primary Charter School, CA

Sunset

The fiery cherry red sky is tinted with bright pink clouds
The breezy clouds and a gassy heated ball;
The sun floats down.
I wish it would never end but it will, it does
Darkness cloaks the Earth like a big cave.

Joelle DiPaolo, Grade 3
Wilchester Elementary School, TX

Rain

Rain splashes on the roof,
Lightning yellow flashes,
Thunder crashes.
Teardrops,
Drip-drop, drip, drop,
Colors of the rainbow,
Jump in puddles — fun!

Ava, Shea, Talia, Mark, Kavvy, and Parker, Kindergarten
The Presentation School, CA

Comets

Comets — not stars, planets or moons
Remnants in space orbiting around the Sun
Dirty snowballs melting like snowmen on a hot day
Racing through the Kuiper Belt and Oort Cloud
Getting pushed around
Halley will be on tour in 2061
I hope that you get to see it.

Jonathan Markowitz, Grade 3
Saigling Elementary School, TX

Comics

I'm trying to think of a topic.
Cuz I love writing comics!
First I grab a paper.
Then I become a creator.
Comics are fun once there done.
You can read them and laugh at them.
You will see, you will laugh at them just like me!

Melodie Yates, Grade 2
Hadley School, CA

What Would We Do Without a Dad?

We wouldn't be fishing!
We wouldn't be to the park!
We would have nightmares of big bad scary sharks!
Nothing would be rad,
I would be sad,
my sister would be mad,
nobody would be glad if we didn't have a dad.

Jayden Myers, Grade 3
Edward Byrom Elementary School, OR

Ants
Small bugs
Holding, marching, crunching
Little little tiny bugs
Insects
Ireland Larson, Grade 1
Highland Park School, MT

Hop
I like to hop on one foot
You need to be careful
I always like to hop on one foot
And I always like to do this...stop
Caden DeSoto, Kindergarten
Legacy Christian Academy, NM

Our Sun
Our sun is a star that shines so bright.
The star twinkles in the midnight light.
Light is a thing that goes in the night.
Night fades in the sun's bright sight.
Jasper Fairchild, Grade 1
Highland Park School, MT

Rhyming
Cat, mat, sat
I like rhyming words a little
Purple, murple, curple
I can make up rhyming words
Cadee Cannon, Kindergarten
Legacy Christian Academy, NM

Seals
Cute loud
Barking, clapping, swimming
Great seals are happy
Sea lions
Jonathon Hoskison, Grade 1
Highland Park School, MT

Horse
Fast runners
eating, running, drinking
pretty animals, fast runner,
Colt
Bridger Burnham, Grade 1
Highland Park School, MT

Twin
The most annoying thing is
when Blair says "Are you awake?"
In the morning Blair says "Let's go
Now!"
Allison Smith, Grade 3
Speegleville Elementary School, TX

Gentoo
Fast runners
Running, sliding, diving
They are fast runners.
Bird
Dillon Cooler, Grade 1
Highland Park School, MT

German Shepherd
Big, black
Walking, chasing, running
The dog chases strangers away.
Bodyguard
Shane Slim, Grade 3
Nenahnezad Community School, NM

Gentoos
Fast swimmers
Swimming, eating, sleeping
They are cool penguins
Birds
Gideon Neff, Grade 1
Highland Park School, MT

The Lake

I sit by the lake feeling the wind whistle past me
the red wooden boat, still in the water
the cranes seemed to dance in the sky
the willow tree's boughs hang low and touch the lake

The carp swim around
in their kingdoms of water and weeds
turtles raise their heads like majestic horses
out of the water they stare

Water lilies bloom
splashes of yellow, white and pink
a disturbance raised them
a frog splashes into the water

A tall beech tree lays long shadows over it
casting out sunlight
on the other side of the lake
a few mallards swim eating duck weed.

Sydney Liao, Grade 3
Top Kids Center, CA

Sports

I like lots of sports, all kinds of sports.
I like basketball more than the other ones.

A basketball is bouncy.
A tennis ball looks like a baseball.

They are different in their colors,
and the way they feel.

Volleyball is more challenging,
more than the other ones.

Bowling is a little bit cool,
but the ball is heavy.

Your bowling ball can be blue,
or it could have yellow stars.
What is your favorite sport?

Jenna Maldonado, Grade 3
H W Schulze Elementary School, TX

Shakira

Shakira likes to sing a pretty song,
with rhyming, it is fun.

Shakira likes to be in the hot son.
Shakira maybe does a beautiful dance
with a nice drum.

Sometimes she can knock you over.
Shakira loves her busy family.

Madyson Garza, Grade 3
H W Schulze Elementary School, TX

What to Do When It Rains?

What to do when it rains?
Let's play some games!
So, my mom and I
Played a game in July.
What kind of game?
I cannot say.
Maybe it was the kind
You play in Tim-Buk-Too.
It was a nice thing to do.

Franklin Huang, Grade 2
Westview School, TX

Snow

I look outside —
a white world
slippery and slick.
I play in the snow.
Snow dances onto my head as
soft as can be.

Aiden Colvin, Grade 2
Gause Elementary School, WA

Chickens

Chickens
soft, beak
walking, laying eggs, flying
feathers, brown
hens

Ethan Goodell, Grade 1
CLASS Academy, OR

Alexis's Summer Surfer

S earched for seals.
U p from the water.
M ovement.
M orning.
E dge.
R ocky beach.

S light.
U pward.
R ain filled the sky.
F ish.
E arly spring.
R oses grew.
S eals.

Alexis Alvarez, Grade 3
Midland Elementary School, CA

I Had a Bad Teacher

I had a bad teacher,
Who had no mind.
It seemed as if
Her heart was blind.

I had a bad teacher,
Who was mean and cruel.
Her only point in life,
Was to rule.

I had a bad teacher,
But it was all a dream.
'Cause if it were real,
I'd wake up and scream.

Natalia Yarbrough, Grade 3
John Hightower Elementary School, TX

Cursive

Cursive
Slanty, curvy
Working, flowing, swerving
Cursive is very beautiful
Writing

Zoe Hernandez, Grade 3
Ygnacio Valley Christian School, CA

Ladybugs
They crawl on the bush
They crawl around in the grass
They are really small

Emily Lonsdale, Grade 3
McDowell Mountain Elementary School, AZ

Blue Jay
Blue, small, can fly high
Eat worms, lives in a small tree
Brownish legs it has

Drake Dannenberg, Grade 3
McDowell Mountain Elementary School, AZ

Hummingbirds
Shiny, pretty bird
Sipping nectar forever
They are so pretty

Aaliyah Flores, Grade 3
McDowell Mountain Elementary School, AZ

Vines
They are green and long.
They help monkeys get across.
They hang on a tree.

Kai Becker, Grade 3
McDowell Mountain Elementary School, AZ

Catfish
Big whiskers and fins
Very poisonous and big
Swimming back and forth.

Brandon Colabianchi, Grade 3
McDowell Mountain Elementary School, AZ

Clouds
Floating in the sky
They are puffy and are white
They are rolling by

Foster Woolbright, Grade 3
McDowell Mountain Elementary School, AZ

Flowers

F ragrance so sweet
L ovely blossoms
O rchids grow
W ater lilies bloom
E ver so beautiful
R ich colors
S ilky petals

Anya Ocampos, Grade 3
Spring Valley Elementary School, TX

Last

I have always been last.
Getting in line, I am last.
Getting my turn, I am last.
Getting a test, I am last.
I am always last.
We just got in line. I am not last.
Last has faded away.

Makenzie Gillette, Grade 3
Spring Valley Elementary School, TX

Tigers

Striking through the woods
Hungry, chomp
Orange as the sun, black as the night
Hungry
Living in the zoo
Sharp white eye

Carter Dixon, Grade 2
Horn Academy, TX

Spring

S weet smell of spring
P iping little birds
R ed roses start to grow
I ncredible time of year
N ice little flowers
G reat, don't you think?

Emma Wakefield, Grade 2
Horn Academy, TX

My Clock

My clock is an octagon,
I put it on my wall,
But it fell down and became a pentagon,
One hand fell far away,
But the other was there.
My dad had to fix it,
In a few days the batteries were gone,
I knew they were old,
My dad got new ones,
Now my clock looks yellow as gold.

Alan Li, Kindergarten
Scholars Academy, CA

Cole

My best friend Cole.
Cool, funny, and fabulous.
He is neat and
his brother is funny.

If I didn't
have him as
a friend I wouldn't
have any friends.
Cole is cool!

Will Scheland, Grade 3
Wilchester Elementary School, TX

My Room

In my room
I snuggle in bed
In my room
My stuffed animals stay
In my room
My room
I will play
In my room
I sleep
All night

Annaka-Joy Bronk, Grade 1
Horn Academy, TX

High Merit Poems – Grades K, 1, 2, and 3

Fun Loving Guy
First name Christopher
Is sporty, lazy, smart
Love dogs, family, friends
Is good at drawing, sports, origami
Feels caring, confident, curious
Needs house, water, food
Wants money, mansion, pool
Fears bad dreams, zombies, ghosts
Likes to eat palabok, Chicharone, Lumpia
Watches Hop, Doe Piece, Family Guy
Is a resident of Ewa Beach, Hawaii
Last name Tenbroeke
Christopher Tenbroeke, Grade 3
Keone'ula Elementary School, HI

Chicks!
Peep peep
They say
when they hatch.
So cute,
so fluffy.

When they grow up
it's time
to start laying eggs.
It's so much fun.
When they hatch
it starts all over!
Brooklyn Lopez, Grade 3
Robinson Elementary School, TX

Hunting
Colton's the name,
I have lots of fame,
and hunting is my game.
I stalk,
pounce,
and purr.
Packed in whiskers
and fur.
Hunting is
a stunt,
skill,
and will.
Colton Helpert, Grade 3
Robinson Elementary School, TX

My Life
First name Warren
is funny, nice, caring
Love bed, family, dog
Is good at games, cooking, school
Feels happy, excited, ready
Needs water, food, family
Wants candy, games, toys
Fears dark, bad dreams, death
Like to eat pizza, salad, yogurt
Watches *Wall-e*, *Spongebob*, *Beyblade*
Is a resident of Ewa beach, USA Hawaii
Last Name Hutchins
Warren Hutchins, Grade 3
Keone'ula Elementary School, HI

Summer
I see bees
and butterflies, birds.
We swim, we play
outside.
We are out of
school.
I'm happy,
we stay at home,
we have fun.
Elianah Locke, Grade 3
Robinson Elementary School, TX

My Dad!
My dad is important to me.
He takes me to places.
We play football together.
He makes me laugh.
We go car washing on the weekend.
He is a smart man.
He is an engineer.
I feel lonely when he goes to China.
I love my dad and he loves me too.
Ebaad Usmani, Grade 3
Islamic School of San Diego, CA

In the Summer
In the summer,
My mom had an idea!
It wasn't a bummer.
"Let's travel," she said.
So she took me with her
To Chicago, Los Angeles, and there
I had a splendid time
Traveling with my mom.
Frankie Torres, Grade 3
Westview School, TX

My Mom and My Homework
I do my homework everyday.
"Please, help me mom," I will say.
Mom comes and looks at my work,
And tells me when I am wrong.
She underlines the information,
Reminds me the letter formation.
I cannot imagine better fun,
Than to do homework with my mom!
Edward Saldaña, Grade 2
Westview School, TX

Fashion Up
I saw a dress
I put it on
I looked pretty
All day long.
I went to the city
And saw a kitty
I drove back to my house
And saw a mouse.
Aubrey Spadachene, Grade 1
Cypress Christian School, TX

Blueberry
I tasted a blueberry,
big and small,
sweet and
sour, soft
and hard.
I could
eat 100
blueberries.
Regan Zohnnie, Grade 2
Nenahnezad Community School, NM

A Day at the Ocean
Beautiful water
Swim with the dolphins
Surf on the waves
Make a sandcastle
Have fun finding sea shells
And a sand dollar, too
It's a beautiful sunset
At the ocean
Abigaile Molander, Grade 3
Legacy Christian Academy, NM

Wind
The wind
sounds like
whoosh and it's
scary and
quiet. It feels
cold and cool.
I see dirt and
trash.
Kacie Yazzie, Grade 2
Nenahnezad Community School, NM

Willie
Sometimes he cuddles up with me
Sometimes he kinda follows me
Every time I get his toy, he goes crazy
His name is Willie
He's my cat
Emilee Oechsner, Kindergarten
Legacy Christian Academy, NM

The Sun
The sun is hot
The hottest thing in the world
It is a star
It gives us heat to the Earth
God made the sun
Andrew Corona, Grade 3
Legacy Christian Academy, NM

High Merit Poems – Grades K, 1, 2, and 3

Beaver

Beaver with such mighty big teeth.
In the river half asleep.
Beaver gets sleepier and sleepier approaching his dam.

5 seconds later…sound asleep.
When Beaver wakes up a whole new day sprouts.

Going out to search for food.
Beaver spots me. He gets scared and swims away.
He comes back later and does not spot me.
Heading to his dam, goes in for the night.
Comes back out tomorrow.

Daniel Sullivan, Grade 3
McDowell Mountain Elementary School, AZ

About Me Sammy!

First name Samantha
Is smart, giving, nice
Love dogs, family, friends
Is good at acting, getting mad, and getting good grades
Feels happy, joyful, loved
Needs family, school supplies, food
Wants money, toys, and a pet
Fears dark, bad grades, ghosts
Likes to eat watermelon, sea weed, chocolate
Watches *Last Song*, *Ghost Hunters*, *SpongeBob*
Is a resident of Ewa Beach, Hawaii
Last name Perez

Samantha Perez, Grade 3
Keone'ula Elementary School, HI

My Pet Dog

My pet dog likes to sprint.
Every day when I come home she runs to me.
I know that she is shy,
Jumping on the couch like a monkey.

Eating quickly like a machine.
Happily jumping on the bed.
When she is hungry she growls.
Sometimes she eats treats instead.

Victoria Nguyen, Grade 3
Oak Park Elementary School, CA

Computers
I like to play games
On the computer
A computer helps you
Learn stuff
I love computers
Computers have electricity
Jose Hernandez, Grade 1
Horn Academy, TX

My Birthday
I am happy
For my birthday
It's the best time of
The year!
Everyone says
HAPPY BIRTHDAY!
Madison Motes, Grade 1
Horn Academy, TX

Springtime
Spring is yellow and pink.
It tastes like a fresh egg,
It sounds like a smooth jazz song,
And smells like fresh lavender.
It looks like a warm sunny day,
Spring makes me feel happy and sweet.
Benjamin Siciliano, Grade 3
Wilchester Elementary School, TX

Comets
Crazy comets orbiting our solar system
A gargantuan dirty snowball
Sweating in the solar wind
Particles falling like grass blowing
Gas and dust slowly turning into a coma
Trailing behind a shrinking ball
Jonathan Cui, Grade 3
Saigling Elementary School, TX

Desert
Endless sea of sand
Dead plants
Ships of the desert walking
Howling rough sand blows in your face
Almost nothing can be seen
But somewhere deep down there is life
Joseph Jeffery, Grade 2
Eagle Springs Elementary School, TX

Baseball
I like baseball
Baseball is fun
Home run!
Single
Triple!
Double!
Jase Schmalz, Grade 1
Horn Academy, TX

Fall
F un to pick
A utumn
L eaves go to the ground
L eaves change colors
Roshen Nair, Kindergarten
CLASS Academy, OR

Fall
F un to pick berries
A utumn
L eaves go to the ground
L eaves change colors
Hannah Nellen, Grade 1
CLASS Academy, OR

Falcons
Fast soaring birds fly
Speeding across the blue sky
Down they dive at prey
Joshua Ikeda, Grade 3
Castleman Creek Elementary School, TX

Winter
I love the winter.
The winter snow is icy.
The snow is melted.
Ariana Conn, Grade 3
Nenahnezad Community School, NM

Nature

Nature is beautiful.
Birds sing high and low melodies.
Bunnies jump on the grass as they look for food.
Plants pop out from the ground, standing tall and beautiful.
Leaves on the trees shine and feel like silk.
Macaws and toucans soar high in the sky.
Sometimes, rain falls from the sky to give water to all.
I love nature!

Fatimah Siddiqah, Grade 3
Islamic School of San Diego, CA

Beautiful Spring

Beautiful spring starts.
How do I know?
Well, the robin chirps.
The deer play.
The flowers blossom.
The sun shines and gets stronger each day.
The snow melts.
Beautiful spring starts.

Amreen Naveen, Grade 3
Islamic School of San Diego, CA

Excited

Children love the sound of the good music.
Whenever it is a soft sound of music.

Children love playing outside on the playground.
Together they help each other when they get hurt.

They like to do talents on the stage.
People love to go see the children's talents.

Angelina Longoria, Grade 3
H W Schulze Elementary School, TX

Black and White Stripes

Zebra
Fast, stripped
Running, eating, drinking,
A very fast animal
Prey

Cameron Washington, Grade 2
Tracy Learning Center - Primary Charter School, CA

Flying Snowflakes

Stars drifting softly through the sky
Puffy silk swerving in the breeze
Sugary cookies waving like ice cream
Flowers spinning like a small mouse
Puffy crystals dancing like birds flying
Twinkling stars shooting through the night
Feathery birds flying like shooting stars
Christmas lights shining when Santa and his reindeer come to visit for cookies!
When you hear the bells, you will know that Santa is coming in his sleigh
Marshmallows tumbling into a warm hot cocoa

Wyatt Tucker, Grade 3
Lolo Elementary School, MT

My Two Dogs

Remy is my dog.
Her fur is as white as fog.
Remy's sister is named Marty.
They both love to party.
Remy and Marty prance and dance.
They always like to take a chance.
They don't like cats.
They're kind of fat.
Sometimes they fight.
Remy always thinks she's right.

Richard Ramayla, Grade 3
St Anthony Immaculate Conception School, CA

Weekends

When the sun is out, I go to the park.
I go inside when it's really dark.
I lost my dog and I want to get another pet,
But my dad said, "Not yet!"
Sometimes I just relax in the pool.
When I don't have any school.
I like to play.
But only in the day.
There's a lot of killer bees
In the big trees.

Patrick Padilla, Grade 3
St Anthony Immaculate Conception School, CA

High Merit Poems – Grades K, 1, 2, and 3

Anthony's Good Life

First name Anthony
Is caring, friendly, nice
Love family, dogs, Xbox 360
Is good at surfing, poker, black jack
Feels shy, happy, excited
Needs water, food, money
Wants new shoes, new clothes, a lot of money
Fears bees, piraña, sharks
Likes to eat chicken, friend noodles, Musubi
Watches Sponge Bob, Spliced, The Lorax
Is a resident of Ewa Beach, Hawaii
Last name Gaballo

Anthony Gaballo, Grade 3
Keone'ula Elementary School, HI

All About Me

First name Jordan
Is lazy, organized, funny
Loves army, my family, and pets
Is good at biking, taking care of my stuff, sports
Feels happy, tired, confident
Needs water, food, milk
Wants a rabbit, parrot, Pomeranian
Fears ghosts, zombies, aliens
Likes to eat steak, macaroni and cheese, pizza
Watches War Horse, Longest Day, D-day
Is a resident of Ewa Beach, Hawaii
Last name Salazar

Jordan Salazar, Grade 3
Keone'ula Elementary School, HI

The Stars

The stars twinkling up,
In black nothing,
Two stars, three stars, a million stars and…
Nothing. Absolutely nothing.
The black nothing,
   has
      been
         sucked
           away.

Isabella Mandeville-Martinez, Grade 2
Robert L Stevens Elementary School, CA

Grace Goodson and MaryGrace McConn
They're nice and happy.
They care for me
And help me through hard times.
When people are mean to me,
They stand up for me.
When someone excludes me,
They tell them it's a free country.
When I cry,
They make me laugh.
That's MaryGrace McConn and Grace Goodson.

Maggie Vierra, Grade 3
Wilchester Elementary School, TX

Nakita
I saw Nakita at the shelter all alone.
I knew what she needed, she needed a home.
She had some bad habits that I knew we could fix
and before I knew it I was teaching her tricks.
I make sure she has food
and that's what keeps my mom and dad in a good mood.
She waits at the gate every morning to say bye
and when I come home from school she's there again to say hi.
She's a beautiful dog now she is happy and free
and I know it's because she came home with me.

Charlize Mazon, Grade 1
Meadows Union School, CA

Appa
Appa is excited when people come in my aunt's house.
He likes to swim in pools.
Runs quickly in the house.
When the dog is so happy he drools.

Nibbling on his doggy food.
Drinking from a bowl of fresh water.
Eating ravenously in the kitchen.
Whenever he is thirsty he acts like an otter.

Vivian Nguyen, Grade 3
Oak Park Elementary School, CA

Christmas Tree

It's Christmas time and I am making some hot chocolate.
I love Christmas because it snows and that's when Santa Claus comes to town.

When it's Christmas, I can open my Christmas presents.
Santa Claus will put candy in my nice stocking.

When I am asleep, he will come to my room and give me a big fluffy puppy for Christmas.

Kathleena Burkett, Grade 3
H W Schulze Elementary School, TX

The Grass

The grass feels watery
The morning dew smells sweet
Aidan looked at me
I hear my feet
The dead grass is dry
The good grass is wet
The birds are singing "Good morning, world!"
And the world says it back

Augustus Guikema, Grade 2
Mosaic Academy, NM

I Love My Family

I love my family and they love me too.
My family is always there for me no matter what.
My mom helps me with my homework.
She feeds me healthy food.
My dad works hard to give us money.
He helps me learn Arabic and the Koran.
My family is irreplaceable.
I love my family.

Omar Eldegwy, Grade 3
Islamic School of San Diego, CA

Colors

Colors
Magical, love
Running, hopping, rolling,
Wonderful, beautiful, dancing, everywhere,
World

Lilly McMahon, Grade 3
Tracy Learning Center - Primary Charter School, CA

Horse
Enchanting horses
Run through the snow silently
They don't know I'm here.

Ainsley Boersma, Grade 3
McDowell Mountain Elementary School, AZ

White Tiger
White tiger in snow
Blends in with snow perfectly.
Magic and pretty.

Gigi Kastner, Grade 3
McDowell Mountain Elementary School, AZ

Owls
Owls hunting at night,
rotating head, night vision.
He is a hunter.

Jacob Pittsenbarger, Grade 3
McDowell Mountain Elementary School, AZ

Dr. Seuss' "The Cat in the Hat"
Dr. Seuss made a rhyming cat
He was being creative
and put it in a hat

Kyle Carlos, Grade 2
Tracy Learning Center - Primary Charter School, CA

Dolphins
Beautiful dolphins
Somersault through the deep sea
With their pretty fins.

Catherine Pham, Grade 3
McDowell Mountain Elementary School, AZ

Mockingbirds
Imitating songs.
Mocking birds are copiers.
Always being loud.

Tyberious Roehrig, Grade 3
McDowell Mountain Elementary School, AZ

High Merit Poems – Grades K, 1, 2, and 3

The Story from the Library

I opened the door to the library and out came books
I opened the books and out came a story
I opened the story and out came an adventure
I opened the adventure and out came a dragon
I opened the dragon and out came treasures
I opened the treasures and out came a map
I opened the map and out came pirates
I opened the pirates and out came a ship
I opened the ship and out came a prisoner
I opened the prisoner and out came a story
I opened the story and out came a book
I closed the book and brought it back to the library.

Natalie Scott, Grade 2
Seattle Jewish Community School, WA

James

First name James
Is funny, nice, shy
Loves mom, beach, dad
Is good at strategy, video games, cooking
Feels happy, sad, angry
Needs water, food, mom/dad
Wants PS3, Skylanders, Infamous 2
Fears Zombies, needles, poisonous snakes
Likes to eat Udon, sakana, dad's meat
Watches Transformers, Rescue Bots, Ninjago
Is a resident of Oahu, Hawaii
Last name Ikeda

James Ikeda, Grade 3
Keone'ula Elementary School, HI

Orange, Yellow, Pink, Red

Orange, Yellow, Pink, Red.
Colors dancing across the sky.
Beauty sparkles all around.
My shadow flows away with the water.
The warm sun sets down.
"Bye," nature calls as rays disappear from sight.
As a moon springs up to greet the night,
I lay there on the cool grass
and picture the sunset of tomorrow night.

Nisarga Ramesh, Grade 3
Medina Elementary School, WA

My Life

First name Matthew
Is sneaky, crazy, disorganized
Loves dogs, family, history
Is good at magic tricks, games, inventing
Feels hyper, excited, scared
Needs food, shelter, water
Wants 6 million dollars, a time machine, a PSP
Fears aliens, zombies, ghosts
Like to eat pears, meat, vegetables
Watches *Metal Eagle*, *Mad*, *Sponge Bob*
Is a resident of Ewa Beach, Hawaii
Last name Munger

Matthew Munger, Grade 3
Keone'ula Elementary School, HI

Personality

First name Ayleen
Is caring, funny, creative
Loves school, running, family
Is good at drawing, running, jump rope
Feels creative, joyful, excited
Needs family, clothes, water
Wants money, family, phone
Fears ghosts, failing, losing my family
Likes to eat Mexican candy, crab, sushi
Watches the *Bee Movie*, *Too Cute*, *Good Luck Charlie*
Is a resident of Ewa Beach, Hawaii
Last name Garcia

Ayleen Garcia, Grade 3
Keone'ula Elementary School, HI

Recess

Recess is fun.
Recess is great.
Recess is something to appreciate.
Recess is something you can have any day.
Recess you can have any time anyway.
Recess is fun.
Recess is great.
I'm so excited.
I can't wait!

Jenna Borucki, Grade 3
Spring Valley Elementary School, TX

When I Get My New Puppy

When I get my new puppy
He will probably be chubby.
I'll want one that runs to me, Understand?
Can you see?
We're going to love him
But won't name him Tim.
That's what I'll do when I get my puppy
And don't forget that he'll be chubby!

Gillian Storey, Grade 1
Cypress Christian School, TX

My Room

My room is nice,
It has books to make you wise,
It has a computer,
In the corner is my red scooter,
I share it with my brother,
There is a picture of my father and mother,
I love my room,
It's the best place on Earth.

Joseph Hua, Kindergarten
Scholars Academy, CA

Transformer

If I were a Transformer,
I would be as strong as a super hero,
I would save people from the evil ones.
The number of bad people in the world would be zero.
I would transform into a car or a robot,
As a car I would go fast as a jet,
As a robot I would destroy the evil.
I would be the best Transformer, I bet.

Gurshaan Pannu, Kindergarten
Scholars Academy, CA

Parrots

Parrots
Colorful birds
Flying, landing, picking
Looking for juicy fruit
Birds

Azeza Clark, Grade 2
Tracy Learning Center - Primary Charter School, CA

Humming Bird

Humming bird as you fly so much time
passes us by, gazing upon your colorful
wings I stand close by. With glistening
eyes and a long sleek beak,
you go from flower to flower making them glow
over my flowers making them glow. Even
the great weather can't stop me from staring
at your radiant rainbow-colored feathers. Humming bird
though you are still small you can do the biggest
things, like make me say, humming bird
please don't go for you see the greatest
in me, and who will let me gaze upon
their colorful wings and long sleek beak?
Oh, humming bird one more thing…do
come back before the end of spring.

Silja Alexander, Grade 3
Spring Creek Elementary School, WY

Lovely

Beautiful, amazing sunsets
Red, orange, yellow, indigo and violet
Lovely fireworks filling the air
Waves crashing in the water
Music, so beautiful to my ears
Stories my Mom tells
Soft grass between my toes
Rain coming down softly on me
A puppy with soft fur
The taste of ice cream m, m, m good
Apples as sweet as pie
The smell of turkey baking on Thanksgiving Day
The smell of popcorn popping
My Mom's homemade banana muffins
Those are the things I love!

Lindsey McMahon, Grade 3
Four Peaks Elementary School, AZ

Playing

I like to play with my baby dolls
Sometimes I play with my Barbie dolls
Cause they have a big house they can go in

Abryanna Marchand, Kindergarten
Legacy Christian Academy, NM

High Merit Poems – Grades K, 1, 2, and 3

The Big Mouse in My House

There is no way to get out of the house
especially with that mouse in the house.
Then what did I hear just right in my ear?
The cat in my house was very close, near.
And, what did that cat say so you say?
The cat said, I'll get rid of that mouse
in your house just using one day.
That mouse was gone in a minute I say.
Then the cat left my house with only one mouse today.

Madison Piazza, Grade 2
Tracy Learning Center - Primary Charter School, CA

My Parents

My parents are important to me.
They have been there for me since I was born.
They wipe my tears when I cry.
They give me medicine when I am sick.
They make food for me.
They give me money when I need it.
They take me to places I love.
They gave me my own room.
I love my parents and they love me.

Reem Awad, Grade 3
Islamic School of San Diego, CA

My First Trip to Greece

I was 8 months old, it was my first time on an airplane.
I was screaming louder than a lion and my mom wanted to kill me.
My dad wanted to kill me because I did make a
scene by kicking and screaming. Then at the end of the
flight I got my first flight certificate to get me quiet
and trust me, it did!

Zoe Sgouros, Grade 2
Annunciation Orthodox School, TX

The Time in My Head

I feel there is a frenzy in my brain with popcorn popping against my ears.
I see notes going crazy, dancing across paper.
I hear a tune in my head like birds singing, owls hooting.
I taste sweet sugarplums, the note in my heart.
I smell butter from the popcorn that's popping.

Katarzyna V. Kwiatkowski, Grade 3
Annunciation Orthodox School, TX

Cobra
A cobra is
One of the
Most
Dangerous snakes
In the world
It is the
Master
Of the
Snakes
Zachary Lewin, Grade 2
Horn Academy, TX

My Family
I love my family a lot.
My family is cool and
My mom and dad love me.
I can do whatever I want when
I do what they want.
I love my family like
They love me.
Loving my family
Is how I spend my days.
Nicole Cronin, Grade 2
Horn Academy, TX

Spring
Spring is when the flowers bloom,
Spring is when the sky is blue.
Spring is when the sun shines,
Spring is when the butterflies fly.
All of this is true,
But the best part is being with you.
Audrey Aceituno, Grade 3
Hadley School, CA

Hat
Hat
Floppy, colorful
sitting, sliding, flying
They are very comfortable
Cap
Jenna Shull, Grade 3
Ygnacio Valley Christian School, CA

The Bee and Me
A flower in a bower
Came a butterfly
Why did the butterfly see a bee?
Why did the bee see me?
Bee, bee, please leave!
Go back to your hive in the tree.
Bye, bye bee.
You can't sting me!
Bzzz
Jeanette Messina, Kindergarten
St Joseph Catholic School, CA

Snow
Snow, it falls,
as winter enters
our human race.
The snow,
as white as a cloud
and as soft as a pillow.
Little sis asks,
when will it leave?
Soon I tell her, soon.
Jordin Martin, Grade 2
Robert L Stevens Elementary School, CA

Sunny Days
I like when it's sunny
It always brightens up my soul
I always see a bunny
Pop into a hole
I love the ice cream on sunny days
That my dad gives me
John Riordan, Grade 2
Mound Valley School, NV

Mom
Mom
black hair, funny
running, jumping, jogging
nice, good
Mommy
Trishna Kumar, Kindergarten
CLASS Academy, OR

High Merit Poems – Grades K, 1, 2, and 3

Sounds
The sound of seagulls
Squawking by the
Sea
The sound of
Basketballs bouncing
On the street the sound of
The ice cream truck
Trotting by
The sound of airplanes
In the sky
The sound of children
Passing by
The sound of bells
Ringing high
The sound of
Tunes in the sky
Saylor Campbell, Grade 2
Horn Academy, TX

Spring
Spring is lovely,
the grass is green,
the flowers bloom,
the soft rain,
the gentle breeze,
Spring is lovely.
Hunter Schmedthorst, Grade 3
Robinson Elementary School, TX

Sunflowers
I love sunflowers,
They look very pretty,
I look at them for hours,
I wish they were all around the city.
They have really big petals,
I want to pick all of them.
I have planted them in pots of metal,
Each one is precious like a gem.
I wish they could play with me,
I wish they could be everywhere I can see,
Sunflowers make me happy!
Rhea Viswanathan, Kindergarten
Scholars Academy, CA

Bailey
B ig
A lways follows me
I love her
L ove
E nergetic and weird
Y oung
Madelyn Carrillo, Grade 1
Horn Academy, TX

Ice Cream
I like ice cream
Ice cream is good
And sweet
And good colors
Ice cream is
My favorite treat!
Grant Griffiths, Grade 1
Horn Academy, TX

Inside Out Day
I wore my shirt on backwards.
I wore my pants on sideways.
I put my socks on inside out.
I wore my shoes the wrong way.
But now I just realized it's
A Saturday!
Alexi Ash, Grade 3
Wilchester Elementary School, TX

Ice Cream
An ice cream sundae
with a cherry on top
chocolate and whipped cream,
gumballs, too.
Evan Corbin, Grade 1
Fir Grove Elementary School, OR

Cherry Trees
The cherry trees bloom
There are lots of cherry trees
The cherry trees grow
Noel Martinez III, Grade 2
Kingwood Montessori School, TX

Monkeys
Sweaty, stinky
Soft, furry, cuddly
Black, brown, fleas, tails
Funny, snickering, laughing, coughing, chuckling

Caroline Parnell, Grade 3
Wilchester Elementary School, TX

Summer
Refreshing, sun screen
Hot, fun, windy
Sunny, colorful, yellow, bright
Laughter, singing, chirping, buzzing, yellow

Ryan McCall, Grade 3
Wilchester Elementary School, TX

Dogs
Trashy, wet
warm, soft, scratchy
brown, white, spotted, striped
barking, howling, crying, screeching, growling

Ava Wylie, Grade 3
Wilchester Elementary School, TX

People and seeds
People go around the world, then find seeds to grow.
They plant the seeds and watch them grow.
Sometimes weeds follow the growth.
Oh, what a wonderful garden.

Connor Able, Grade 3
Wilchester Elementary School, TX

Scorpions
They have a curved tail.
They are very poisonous.
Do not sit on them!

Lance Willim, Grade 3
McDowell Mountain Elementary School, AZ

High Merit Poems – Grades K, 1, 2, and 3

Thanksgiving Day
Thanksgiving day!
Hooray!! Hooray!!
We eat turkey and pie,
We're so happy we cry,
Hip-hip hooray!
It's Thanksgiving day!
Brian Reeves, Grade 3
The School at St George Place, TX

Imagination
A bear is like a fluffy rabbit.
Spaghetti is like a playing jump rope.
A marshmallow is like a sweet lollipop.
An octagon is like a red stop sign.
An oval is like a white egg.
And a cube is like a birthday present.
Alexandra Uribe, Grade 3
Elder Creek Elementary School, CA

My Home
My home is full of love.
We love each other.
We respect each other.
My home keeps me safe and warm.
It is a peaceful place.
My home is very special.
Ibrahim Helmy, Grade 3
Islamic School of San Diego, CA

Hamsters
Hamsters,
Cuddly, cute, little,
Fun, playful
My hamster
Cookie,
The best.
Isabella Tomas, Grade 3
Goethe International Charter School, CA

Hunter
H ilarious
U ltimate
N eedless
T all
E xplosive
R apid
Hunter Galimi, Grade 3
Little Oaks School, CA

Amazing Mom
Nice, sweet, loving,
Respectful, gives me lots of love.
Best in the world…
Has courage
Never gives up.
Strong!!!
Steven McDonald, Grade 3
Wilchester Elementary School, TX

So Much Depends Upon
So much depends upon
if my pony feels
happy, sad, good or bad.
Then I can ride.
Zoe Sexauer, Grade 1
Fir Grove Elementary School, OR

Dinosaurs
Some dinosaurs can fly
High above the sky.
Every day dinosaurs fight,
To show their might.
Carlos Herrera, Grade 2
St Helen Catholic School, CA

Snow
I love snowy days.
Falls, cold, soft, white, gray, clouds.
It is cold outside.
Renae Skeet, Grade 3
Nenahnezad Community School, NM

Love
Love is always good.
It is sweet and nice each day.
Love cannot pass you.
Emma Williams, Grade 3
Warren Elementary School, OR

A Celebration of Poets – West Grades K-3 Spring 2012

Friends

Friends are nice, friends are fun,
Friends are always playing in the sun.
Friends will always be with you.
Friends will even sometimes give you a tissue.
Friends are good, friends are sweet,
Friends might even give you a treat.
When I am mad, when I'm holding a grudge,
I can always have a hug...
From my friends!

Alexis Janousek, Grade 3
Wilchester Elementary School, TX

History

Betsy Ross sewed the flag
Paul Revere gave a warning
Both were done early in the morning
Helen Keller was brave and fought through her problems
Jackie Robinson had it rough
But Rosa Parks was tough
She sat down on the wrong bus
Now you know some history
Next time share it all with me

Sophia Jegi, Grade 3
Wilchester Elementary School, TX

Flowers

Flowers are blue
Laughing flowers in the wind
Orange flowers are beautiful
We love flowers
Imaginary flowers are so cute
Running and laying in flowers
Such a beautiful world
Alhamdulilah

Fatima Erriche, Grade 1
Islamic School of Muslim Educational Trust, OR

Pirate

There was a pirate
The pirate was looking for the treasure chest
In the chest there was a magic wand.

Donovan MacDonald, Grade 2
Whatcom Discovery School, WA

Marina

The wind howling
Wailing like a ghost would
The boats thump, thump, thumping against the dock
The brown water rippling
The dock boards creaking
This is the marina
What a wonderful place to be

Sophie Trammell, Grade 2
St John's School, TX

What Is a Book?

Can I sit on a book? Can I flip pages in a
book? Does a book have pictures? Does a book
have a cover? Does a book have numbers?
Does a book have words? Can I read a book?
Does a book have arms and legs? Can a book
talk? Can a book make you want to scream out
loud? What can a book do?

Meera West, Grade 2
Annunciation Orthodox School, TX

Flowers and Weeds

Flowers
Pretty, cut
Waving, flowing, planting
Root, leaves, stem, harmful
Sucking, sticking, growing
Green, mean
Weeds

Isabella Sousa, Grade 3
Tracy Learning Center - Primary Charter School, CA

Mom and Dad

Mom
Pretty, busy
Telling, cooking, dressing
Dresses, shoes, work, tough
Working, driving, eating
Cool, smelly
Dad

William MacGregor, Grade 3
Tracy Learning Center - Primary Charter School, CA

Trucks

Truck
Hard, metal
Running, turning, driving
Bed, hook, shade, fan
Hooking, heating,
Flat, big
Trailer

Cody Hays, Grade 2
Tracy Learning Center - Primary Charter School, CA

Books

I love books.
They are so wonderful.
They are so interesting.
They are so informative.
They are so suspenseful.
They are full of drama, action, and adventure.
I love books.

Hamza Thange, Grade 3
Islamic School of San Diego, CA

Stars/Planet

Stars
Bright, beautiful
Sparkling, shining, twinkling
Shapes, space, Jupiter, Mars
Rotating, spinning, rolling
Big, small
Planet

Paige Faaborg, Grade 3
Tracy Learning Center - Primary Charter School, CA

Unnamed

Beyblade
Red, blue
Spinning, hitting, bumping
Pisces, Trigger, Slinger, Flamerebra
Playing, sharing, battling
Green, yellow
Arena

Marshall Conner, Grade 2
Tracy Learning Center - Primary Charter School, CA

High Merit Poems – Grades K, 1, 2, and 3

Pancakes
Pancakes
You can put
Blueberry
On your pancakes
Pancakes are good
To eat
Arthur Tang, Grade 1
Horn Academy, TX

The Wind
The wind slams my door.
I jump up.
It opens and shuts.
Opens and shuts.
I close my door and lock it shut.
And I do my work in peace.
Jenna Patton, Grade 2
Grand Ridge Elementary School, WA

Halloween
Halloween is the color orange.
It tastes like candy
It sounds like creepy crawlers
It smells like M&M's
It looks like a dark forest
It makes me feel good
Cade Parnell, Grade 3
Wilchester Elementary School, TX

Ladybugs
Ladybugs I like a lot.
They are black and red.
They come out when it's hot.
I think about them in my head.
Then I let it go.
And I go to bed!
Aylissia Ramirez, Grade 2
Hadley School, CA

A Friend
I like my friend.
He is funny and silly.
I play and laugh with him.
He listens to me.
He teaches me cool moves.
I like my friend.
Ali Khan, Grade 3
Islamic School of San Diego, CA

Who Am I?
Furry creatures from here to there,
Scurrying, scurrying everywhere.
My fur can be white, black, or brown,
Although I will never give a frown.
Try to guess what I am,
You never will, you'll be shut like a clam.
Ava Trilling, Grade 3
Goethe International Charter School, CA

So Much Depends Upon
So much depends upon
A wish I had
A cup of ice
That I would drink.
Peyton Taylor, Grade 1
Fir Grove Elementary School, OR

Night
It drops silently
on the valley
It reminds me
of my favorite blanket
Aviva Nathan, Grade 1
Rio Grande School, NM

Oversized Hamster
Fluffy, fluffy, cute
I am small and have big eyes
Hmm…what could I be?
Niko Zurek, Grade 3
Goethe International Charter School, CA

Tornado
Black clouds fill the sky.
The wind begins to blow hard.
The tornado spins.
Nesto Thomas, Grade 3
Nenahnezad Community School, NM

A Celebration of Poets – West Grades K-3 Spring 2012

Secrets

Secrets, secrets are no fun,
they can really hurt someone.

Telling secrets is not very nice,
especially when a friend might pay the price.

When a secret is whispered in an ear,
you never know who might shed a tear.

If you want to tell a secret, think twice before you do,
because you never know, the secret might be about you!

Stephen Ordorica, Grade 2
St Joseph Catholic School, CA

Christmas

Christmas is the day Jesus was born.
Kids playing in the cold snow
with lots of love and the kids filling with joy.

Santa is coming with lots of cool presents
and lots of kids to enjoy Christmas spirit.

At night on Christmas day stars flash
with a bright yellow color.
Kids ask their friends to come out to play with snowmen,
and they will have snowball fights with laughter and happiness.

Angelo Olivarez, Grade 3
H W Schulze Elementary School, TX

Love

One day something came magically to relax me.
It was a sunny summer day.

The sun was hot, and the sand was cool.
I was excited with lots of happiness.

I brought my pets, but they seemed sad.
Then I knew what to do to cheer them up.

To cheer them up,
I gave them a loving hug.

Dristen Casias, Grade 3
H W Schulze Elementary School, TX

Sister

My sister smells good
She has a great sense of humor.
My sister loves me and I love her.
Tomorrow is my sister's birthday.
My sister is so nice to everybody.
I am going to get my sister a sneaker for her birthday.

Salma Al-Bawani, Grade 3
Islamic School of Muslim Educational Trust, OR

Fresh Air

When I took my first breath it was Washington air
Then my family moved from there
We moved to California before I was one
Then my grammy decided to come
It doesn't matter if we live here or there...
As long as my family can breathe the fresh air!

Caroline Roche, Grade 1
St Joseph Catholic School, CA

Come with Me to the Arctic Tundra

See the plants growing in the soggy ground,
and the caribou migrating south.
Hear the frigid wind blowing so hard,
and the crunch of the snow when you step on it.
Feel the flowers are frozen on your legs,
and the feeling of sinking in the snow.

Valerie Marin, Grade 3
A E Arnold Elementary School, CA

Thunder

It crackles and rumbles
If it hits me I will tumble
Then I will mumble
Till the storm crumbles

Jacob Yu, Grade 3
Tracy Learning Center - Primary Charter School, CA

Roses

Red and beautiful
Peaceful, quiet and lovely
Red, pink, and yellow

Sophia Pellegrino, Grade 3
McDowell Mountain Elementary School, AZ

My Little Sister
My little sister is very sweet,
But sometimes is not very neat.

She fills my heart with joy,
But makes too much noise!

She draws on the wall,
Then on her baby doll.

She is so sporty,
But not a shorty!

She never takes the blame,
So, I have to be ashamed.

Even though she is not very neat or sweet,
I still love my little sissy!
Reagan Dopp, Grade 3
St John's Episcopal Day School, TX

Happy New Year
New Year is coming
Everyone is celebrating
Fireworks to see
Dancers with elegant dances

I make a wish
But it is not a fish

I wish the nature natural
I wish people healthy

I wish the world peaceful

Before the poem ends
I wish you
Happy New Year of 2012
Nerissa Liu, Grade 1
St Thomas the Apostle School, CA

Zoo
I like to go to the zoo.
I hope you do too.
I like to go every day.
I hope it's not a long way.
Sophia Alcazar, Grade 2
St Helen Catholic School, CA

Snowflakes
Snowflakes are bright
Snowflakes are cool
They are white
Freezing cold winter
Penelope Tucker, Grade 1
Horn Academy, TX

Snow
Snow is falling;
the sun is hiding;
the flowers are dying;
the snow is falling.
Devak Singh, Grade 3
Jacob Wismer Elementary School, OR

At the Beach
Waves lapping against the shore
Sun shining on the bay
Beautiful sunset in the sky
I wish I could stay
Sophia Dex, Grade 3
Medina Elementary School, WA

Winter
Winter is so cool
Cool as ice and snow
Snow is white
White is winter
Blaine Spears, Grade 3
Spring Valley Elementary School, TX

High Merit Poems – Grades K, 1, 2, and 3

All in Outer Space!
Comets, asteroids, and meteorites too whizzing past you
Mercury, Venus, Earth, Mars, Jupiter, Saturn, Uranus, Neptune,
And there goes the dwarf planet Pluto all orbiting around the
sun, stars, constellations—very fun to see, and there goes
our only light at night, our bright glowing moon…All in outer space!

Veronica Hsu, Grade 3
Medina Elementary School, WA

Snakes
The snakes are sometimes fakes,
They are fast to get their prey,
They get animals in the tropical forest,
They fight and they might bite,
They can squeeze you and they make you die.

Yadel Estrada, Grade 2
Mesa Vista Elementary School, TX

A Tree
I am tall and I have leaves. Some animals
live in me. There are different kinds of me.
I hold apples, cherries, peaches, and mangoes. People pick them from me.
My blood is sap. People hang rope swings from me.
I am in people's backyards and I am in woods and forests also.

Alexander Smith, Grade 2
East Hill Elementary School, WA

Easter Bunny
The Easter Bunny brings joy to kids'
faces by leaving baskets full of toys at their doors. But,
what I don't like about the Easter Bunny's rules is that he
has to go home after he delivers all the baskets. Gee I
just wish he could stay longer next year, I just wish.

Tristan Raz, Grade 3
Edward Byrom Elementary School, OR

Stars
S aturn and stars and all,
T hrough the telescope I see you,
A ll around you I can see space galore,
R unning away in the morning, and peeking out at night,
S tars and planets are in space…now you know!

Claire Ku, Grade 3
Edward Byrom Elementary School, OR

Blue

Blue is the ocean water
Blue is the sound of waves
Blue is the feeling of snow
Blue is the smell of blueberry bubble gum
Blue is the taste of snowflakes
Blue is the sound of waves crashing together
And blue is the color of smoothness and soft snow

Hailey Shaw, Grade 3
South Bosque Elementary School, TX

Sunflowers

I like sunflowers,
They smell nice,
I planted them myself,
They look pretty at sunrise,
I water them every day,
They are big and yellow,
My entire family loves to watch them grow.

Ishani Kumar, Kindergarten
Scholars Academy, CA

Sisters and Brothers

Sister
Sweet, mean
Shopping, texting, drawing
Make-up, boys, food, jobs
Eating, sleeping, playing
Mean, handsome
Brother

Alaina Pelican, Grade 3
Tracy Learning Center - Primary Charter School, CA

How Pictures Really Come Alive

How pictures really come alive, I'm not really sure they do, but my friend never lies and she told me so, but I'm still wondering if it's her imagination. She told me pictures come alive. She said dogs and cats can come alive, chasing each other around the grocery store!! I really don't believe so but maybe it's true!

Elizabeth McGee, Grade 2
Annunciation Orthodox School, TX

High Merit Poems – Grades K, 1, 2, and 3

Flower
Iris or rose,
Those colors brighten the future like a color wheel,
A sun with petals called sunflower,
They sprout with joy that is contagious,
some bloom some rot and stay in the same spot,
They represent love,
sitting by a gravestone,
Flower never leaves and instead makes you feel graceful,
Flower I won't see you again 'til Spring.
Grace Abawe, Grade 3
Spring Creek Elementary School, WY

Best Friends Rock!
B est friends should be supportive.
E xtra giant-hearted!!!
S uper really funny!!!
T easing never started!

F riendship is very important!
R eally super great!!!
I love how it works out.
E xtra sweet playmate!!!
N ever ever do friends give up!
D o or don't then done!!!
S tick together, work it out!!!

R unning on the run!
O h! So great! I will faint!
C locks I hate! I'm so late!
K ill the hate and just wait!!
Madelyn Chance, Grade 3
Woodway Elementary School, TX

The Life in the Land of Mud
The yellow wheeled sun turns round, as the sneaky snake slithers on the dark mud. The loud rainbow rooster observes the green-yellow snake as it wiggles on and off the path. The weird-eyed hen strolls past the clucking rooster, and spots the purple and pink pig. This is all underneath the sewer-colored sky in the land of mud.
Everett Adkins, Grade 3
Annunciation Orthodox School, TX

Super Bowl
S aints
U p by 20
P atriots
New **E** ngland
R eally real

B oring, not
O rderly, organized
W inners
L osers
Kaitlin Powers, Grade 3
South Bosque Elementary School, TX

Spring Beach
S pring time is fun time.
P eople like to see seals.
R ocks help the seals laying in the sun.
I like to watch things.
N ight time seals sleep.
G randdads are the best.

B oys and girls rock.
E scaping is cool.
A ll seals eat fish.
C arefully I pet the seal.
H ow great seals are.
Oliver Davidson, Grade 3
Midland Elementary School, CA

Rainbows

Once there were rainbows in the sky,
bright colors like red, orange, blue and violet purple,
just staying there like wonderful pink clouds,
in the sky so high.
When I see the rainbow,
I think about the colors,
like red for cherries,
yellow for bananas,
orange for oranges,
green for grapes,
blue for blueberries
and violet purple for cakes.
See the rainbow and wish
for good luck!

Jocelyne Chiquet Torres, Grade 2
Robert L Stevens Elementary School, CA

Alyssa's Life

First name Alyssa
Is sporty, caring, artistic
Love God, animals, biking
Is good at drawing, crafts, singing
Feels blessed, happy, lazy
Needs my friends, my family, water
Wants a dog, money, nook
Fears, zombies, ghosts, clowns
Likes to eat spam and rice, Mahi Mahi, Poke
Watches Punk'd, Glee, Hawaii 5-0
Is a resident of Ewa Beach, Hawaii
Last name Santiago

Alyssa Santiago, Grade 3
Keone'ula Elementary School, HI

Love

When you hear those words
"I love you," it just makes you want to jump.
You want to give love all you have and wrap it up with lace.
You want to hug it and say it back and tell it all your secrets.
Because when it is said, you trust that they meant it.
You want to give that person a million things like cards and best of all, love.
You want to give that person your best poem and I think this one will do.

Caroline Clark, Grade 3
Wilchester Elementary School, TX

High Merit Poems – Grades K, 1, 2, and 3

Oceans

Oceans, soft sand, the sea creatures in the salty water.
Watching the people do creative stuff in the water.

The water tastes like salt, and feeling the water hit you
seems like the waves are going to knock you down.

When the soft sand is wet, it feels like silk.
Kids love making big sand castles
and they make them look so fantastic.

I want to tell them to make another one.

Luis Garcia, Grade 3
H W Schulze Elementary School, TX

All About Patrick

First name Patrick
Is smart, lazy, funny
Loves games, school, basketball
Is good at math, origami, basketball
Feels happy, excited, sad
Needs water, money, family
Wants Suduko, card games, bunny
Fears getting an "F" on a test, get "O" score on worksheet, ghosts
Likes to eat sushi, yakiniku, soba noodles
Is a resident of Ewa Beach, Hawaii
Last name Yamaguchi

Patrick Yamaguchi, Grade 3
Keone'ula Elementary School, HI

Me and My Life

First name Skye
Is funny, organized, awesome
Love sister, mom and dad, aunty tiff
Is good at volleyball, basketball, baseball
Feels happy, sad, confused
Needs water, food and clothes, family
Wants taria, birthday gifts, conches monster
Like to eat steak, pizza, shrimp
Watches *Disney Channel*, *Hawaii 5-0*, *Austin and Ally*
Is a resident of Ewa Beach, Hawaii
Last name Kanamu

Skye Naki-Kanamu, Grade 3
Keone'ula Elementary School, HI

Family
Family can be mean,
Can make it nice,
Family can be aggressive,
Not always smart,
But you can
Make it better by
Being a loving child,
Sharing,
Not hurting feelings
And loving your family
With extra care.
Xavier Ramos, Grade 2
Robert L Stevens Elementary School, CA

Airplanes
Airplanes are big
Some carry over
208 passengers
Watch for big things
In the sky up high
They look very little
As they ZOOM through
Through the sky
Out of the airport
And through the sky
In another airport it comes.
Maxim Kirillov, Grade 2
Horn Academy, TX

Monster Truck
I love trucks
and monster trucks most
every truck is cool
do you think it's so
I like every truck
trucks are the best
they have a cab
they have a tank
they have wheels
they are as strong as cars
Rudy Bennett, Grade 3
Whatcom Discovery School, WA

The Earth
We live on Earth,
There's more water than land on Earth.
The North Pole and South Pole are cold,
Space is around Earth,
There are more planets than our Earth,
But none are like our Earth,
We have to keep it nice and neat.
Vinay Singamsetty, Kindergarten
Scholars Academy, CA

The Bear in the Woods
There once was a bear,
He lived in the woods.
He didn't like his hair.
So he wore his hood.
Then he went to a parlor,
He got his hair done.
And all he gave them was a dollar.
Tony Stevens, Grade 1
Cypress Christian School, TX

Love
Children love playing outside.
When they go outside,
They get excited.

They love playing outside.
Sometimes they hurt themselves,
And they get sad.
Mia Esquivel, Grade 3
H W Schulze Elementary School, TX

My 4 Dogs
Are my 4 dogs playful? Yes!
Are my 4 dogs friendly? Yes!
Are my 4 dogs wild? Yes!
Are my 4 dogs always hungry? Yes!
Are my 4 dogs slobbery? Yes!
Do I love my 4 dogs?
Yes! I love my 4 dogs.
Berkley Bragg, Grade 2
Annunciation Orthodox School, TX

High Merit Poems – Grades K, 1, 2, and 3

Watching Butterflies
Watching butterflies
Is fun
Because you get
To see the colors
Of them
All red
Orange
Blue
Black and
Purple
It's so much fun
To run and jump while
You watch them
Flutter by
Suzanne Lee, Grade 1
Horn Academy, TX

This Is Mine
This is my Wii
It is black
It is old
No one can attack

This is my Wii
It is so cool
It is so awesome
If you play, you are not a fool

This is my Wii
It has cool games
It is so wicked
It has so much fame
Kusal Pedarla, Grade 1
CLASS Academy, OR

Elephants
Elephants
Really big
Eating, swimming, amazing
Great wonderful African animals
Mammals
Katheryn Dowell, Grade 1
Highland Park School, MT

Math
Octagons
Parallelograms
Math is fun for everyone
Addition, subtraction
Times, multiplication
Nonagons, rhombus
Patterns, number lines
Time, money
Math is everywhere
Caitlyn McConnell, Grade 2
Horn Academy, TX

Dogs
Dogs are fluffy
Dogs are silly
Dogs are fun
Dogs wait
To have food dropped
On the floor
And
Who knows what
Dogs will do next!
Sasha Bailey, Grade 2
Horn Academy, TX

Halloween
When is Halloween?
When creepy ghosts scare
And freaky werewolves howl.
When ugly witches fly
And nasty mummies run.
Then it's Halloween!
Alyssa Monfiero, Grade 3
A E Arnold Elementary School, CA

Peace
P erfect always.
E nd a fight.
A lways be nice.
C an't be mean.
E veryone loves each other.
Kaia Wolfe, Grade 3
Broderick Montessori School, CA

Earth

Earth has many oceans.
Earth has many pieces of land.

Earth has lots of peace.
It has many stores.

It has lots of different animals.
It has lots of people.

We have lots of money for different things.
We have different kinds of food, and we have cars.

And most of all we have many friends,
And lots of family to keep us company.

Daitlyn Zuniga, Grade 3
H W Schulze Elementary School, TX

Watching

W atching seals is fun.
A pup seal is a baby seal.
T eaching a seal is fun.
C omparing pups and seals is hard.
H appy seals are nice seals.
I love seals because they're important to me.
N ice seal are cute seals.
G ood seals are jolly seals.

S pring is the time for seals to come out.
E very seal loves to play in the spring.
A ll seals are cute.
L ess seals come back safely.
S ave the seals and they will be happy seals.

Breawna Van Den Berg, Grade 3
Midland Elementary School, CA

Captain Maniac

There once was a pirate named Captain Maniac
For the rest of his life he will be a brainiac
He has a pet cat
The cat eats his friend's rat
His friend's name is Pack

Sashank Meka, Grade 2
CLASS Academy, OR

High Merit Poems – Grades K, 1, 2, and 3

Winter
Winter is white
It tastes like hot chocolate
It sounds like wood crackling
It smells like fire
Looks like families having fun in the snow
Makes me feel warm inside

Caroline Emery, Grade 3
Wilchester Elementary School, TX

Rivers
You can see rivers connected to lakes,
You can see rivers under bridges,
You can call a river a stream,
Rivers can be long,
Rivers can also be short,
I like rivers because I can sail a boat in a river.

Henry Li, Kindergarten
Scholars Academy, CA

Summer
S wimming often
U mbrellas needed
M aking crafts
M adeline cookies
E ating sweets
R unning around

Julia Yanke, Grade 3
Tracy Learning Center - Primary Charter School, CA

Top of the Tree
Far up high, far up in the sky
A gentle robin hops on a branch in an oak tree in Texas.
A peaceful leaf falls, gliding down slowly until it hits the ground.
Even though all appears peaceful, monsters and war are soon to come.

Richard Jacky, Grade 3
Annunciation Orthodox School, TX

A Puppy
They are very cute.
They could be gold, tan, or brown.
They could be fluffy.

Madysen Mah-Bishop, Grade 2
Tracy Learning Center - Primary Charter School, CA

Bright Star

Twinkle, twinkle, I see you bright star,
Hiding in the sky so far.

You are shiny, yellow, and bright so high in the sky,
Sometimes I confuse you for a firefly.

Your light guides us like a shining beacon,
Your shining glow will tell us that night has begun.

When your glistening twinkle fades away,
Out comes a brand new day.

Olivia Sorce, Grade 3
St John's Episcopal Day School, TX

Come with Me to the Desert

See the snakes slithering
to eat their prey
and the mammals drooling and looking for water to drink.
Hear the rattlesnake rattling
so it means a warning
and the cracking eggs
of a new life to begin.
Feel the prickly cactus
when you go to the desert
and the dusty sand
when the wind blows.

Matalina Levi, Grade 3
A E Arnold Elementary School, CA

Kids

Kids getting out of school,
Can't wait to hang out and be cool!

Boys playing football,
And girls playing softball.

Some kids play soccer and say I'm dull,
And others shout GOAL!

Some kids wish the papers at school were burned,
But others wish they had learned!

Tony Trad, Grade 3
St John's Episcopal Day School, TX

The Brown Tribe People Hunting

The brown tribe people hunting, running, bears here.
People hunting, sprinting, coyotes there.
People hunting, jogging, deer over there.
The brown tribe people hunting quick,
hawks by a totem pole!
People hunting everywhere.
The night sky with a sun still in it.
It's very odd here.
The faces on screaming
totem poles reach to the solid black sky.
The rocky outcrop gleams across the land.
The peaks reach to the tip top of the sky.

Gunnar Brown, Grade 3
Annunciation Orthodox School, TX

What is a Book?

Is a book chapter or picture?
Is a book nonfiction or fiction?
Is a book big or small?
Does a book have pictures or photographs?
Is a book old or new?
Does a book have words?
Is there a book called Friends are Nice by author Natalie Allen?
What
is
a
Book?

Natalie Allen, Grade 2
Annunciation Orthodox School, TX

Christmas Is in the Air

You can smell it when the gingerbread
men pop out of the oven.
You can taste it when the pomegranate pie
whooshes down your throat.
You can hear it when the
church bells ring in your ears.
You can see it when the presents are placed
under the scented Christmas tree.
You can feel it when the magic falls
from the Christmas sky.

Kate E. Hada, Grade 3
A E Arnold Elementary School, CA

A Plant
The important thing about a plant
is that it is green.
It is true that they have leaves, soil, and seeds.
You can touch it, feel it, and see it.
They are everywhere in the world.
But the important thing about
a plant is that it is green.

Emma Castro, Grade 2
Vista Square Elementary School, CA

Heroes
Mom is my favorite word in the whole world.
She loves me when I am good or bad.
She picks me up when I am felling sad.
There is nothing my mom can't do.
My mom is a hero.
Your mom is a super hero to you.
So thanks mom for the love you give.

Joygavion Jones, Grade 3
Tatum Primary School, TX

Colors
Bright colors, dark colors, neon colors, dull colors
yellow, peach, orange, green
colors, colors, colors
leaves, books, rubies, grass
colors everywhere
everything has a color
even you

Aakanksha Deb, Grade 3
Medina Elementary School, WA

Baseball
Baseball
Exciting, unexpected
Hitting, fielding, running
Crack! I run as I watch the ball go over the fence.
Amazing, earning, talking
Fun, sweating
Player

Ethan Gadbois, Grade 3
Horn Academy, TX

Every Time My Heart Beats

Every time my heart beats a second passes, a minute passes
Every time my heart beats an hour passes, a day passes

Every time my heart beats a flower blooms
Every time my heart beats a petal falls

Every time my heart beats someone gets out of bed
Every time my heart beats someone falls asleep

Every time my heart beats a baby is born
Every time my heart beats death is in the air

Every time my heart beats I pray someone believes in the Lord
Every time my heart beats I praise the Lord

Every time my heart beats

Sequoia Ayers, Grade 3
Lake Almanor Christian School, CA

Light

Oh light please shine tonight
as the stars glimmer bright.
Light, Light, Light is what I seek, so I can peek
in the darkest temples that are unique
and see the ancient treasures
that can only be seen by the
stars that glimmer bright.

Collin Golden, Grade 3
Edward Byrom Elementary School, OR

Surprise Box

I was in my yard digging a deep hole near the sea.
Then my shovel hit something hard.
Crash!
Into the hole I reached to pull out a metal box as small as a lunch box.
In the sand and dirt near the box I looked for a key but I could not find it.
Sarah the seal washed up on shore and I helped her back to sea.
She said she saw the key in the sea.
Sarah the seal brought the key from the water.
In the box was a pot of gold and a note that said,
"Spend this surprise with your family."

Olivia Pieper, Grade 2
Annunciation Orthodox School, TX

Horses
While they run they're in a different world
They run wild and they run fast
They hear the wind against their ears
They hear their hooves clip-clopping on the ground
They feel their hearts beating fast
They feel their legs aching in pain
They see the trees, a blur as they run
They see the sun directly in their eyes
Blinding them as they run
Finally they stop and everything is still,
They are back to the real world

Reese Ramirez, Grade 3
Horn Academy, TX

Bald Eagle
I see a bald eagle flying with a seagull.
The bald eagle flies away from the seagull.
Are they no longer friends?
Why is the bald eagle
Being mean to the seagull?
I wish they were still friends.
Or are they just playing tag?
That was it!
Now I know!
They were just playing a game.
They are still friends the same.

Kaelen Lambert, Grade 1
Woodcrest School, CA

This Is Mine
This is my sister
She is very cute
She loves to play and she's never mute

This is my sister
She is awesome fun
She wanders around the house and sometimes, she runs

This is my sister
She is always thinking of trouble
She doesn't like to sleep and loves to play with bubbles

Noopur Barve, Grade 2
CLASS Academy, OR

High Merit Poems – Grades K, 1, 2, and 3

The Sun

The sun is yellow,
the sun is yellow.
So play under the
sun. I like the sun.
I love the sun. The
sun loves me. I like to play
in the sun.
Sophia Habib-Dueben, Grade 1
Jefferson Elementary School, WA

Boys and Girls

Boys
Cool, naughty
Chasing, fighting, laughing
Games, soccer balls, Barbies, lipstick
Reading, giggling, shopping
Fancy, pretty
Girls!
Wayo Mora, Grade 3
St John's Episcopal Day School, TX

Monkeys

My, look at those
Opposable toes
Never falling off the tree,
Keeping their grip at
Every branch and stick,
You'd never know we're related,
See?
Catalina Lind, Grade 3
Woodway Elementary School, TX

The Closet

When I hear laughs
and other eerie sounds
coming from the closet,
I get frightened.
What kind of monsters
are living
in my mind?
Trenton Hamilton, Grade 2
Gause Elementary School, WA

My Dad

He has a nice beard,
Is full of fun.
Dad is taller than mom
And very nice to us,
Plus...
  He's the best
  Dad ever!
Katherine Simpson, Grade 3
Woodway Elementary School, TX

My Mom

My mom is the best.
She is kind.
She never quits helping us.
She drives me to school every day.
She cooks for me every day.
She takes good care of me.
My mom loves me and I love her.
Mikail Fontanez, Grade 3
Islamic School of San Diego, CA

The Mysterious Thing

The arrow of every bow,
The start of time,
The start of taste,
I may be in a commercial,
What am I?

Answer: The letter T
Drew Pinkstaff, Grade 3
Woodway Elementary School, TX

Eraser

Eraser
Square, white
Erasing, coloring, wiping
Paper, homework, school, sharpener
Coloring, writing, creating
Yellow, wooden
Pencil
Dayshell Licona, Grade 3
St John's Episcopal Day School, TX

Page 135

Seal of Pups

W hile I was reading the book it was quite cool.
I n the spring the grandson got an idea for the pup to get food.
N ight is when they go to sleep.
T he seal likes to eat fish.
E arly in summer Ben watched the pup swim in the sea.
R ocks are where the seals lay down.

Thabita Sandoval, Grade 3
Midland Elementary School, CA

Spring

Spring is when birds start to sing
Flowers start to bloom
It is beautiful I assume
Alarm clocks go a-ling a-ling
Spring is when butterflies spread their wings
Spring is everything

Alexa Doyle, Grade 3
South Bosque Elementary School, TX

Blue

Blue is the color of the sadness in your eyes.
Blue is the gleam of a sapphire.
Blue is the feeling of water in your hands.
Blue is the spots of a robin's egg.
Blue is the patter of raindrops falling.
And blue is a color that is filled with life and a blaze of fire.

Eubin Shim, Grade 3
South Bosque Elementary School, TX

Fifty Magnificent States

States are so beautiful
States are so different,
That's why the states are…
MAGNIFICENT!!!

Iza Rae Konings, Grade 3
Santa Fe School for the Arts and Sciences, NM

Angel Fish

I like to eat fish.
My shape is triangular.
I am colorful.

Madison Frush, Grade 3
McDowell Mountain Elementary School, AZ

High Merit Poems – Grades K, 1, 2, and 3

My Dog Jazz

Jazz likes to jump on the bed.
He quickly runs around to eat.
He slowly goes under the blanket.
Sometimes he goes under the sheet.

Jumping on people when they come,
On the couch he likes to jump.
Knees arms legs and shoulders
Are things that he will bump.

Eating through the food like a wild animal.
Acting like he hasn't eaten in a year.
Chomps the leftovers on my plate,
I think he may eat a deer.

Licking his paw very loud,
It annoys my mom and me.
When my mom's on the phone it's not hard to hear.
Sometimes we want everyone to see.

I love my dog a lot.
He comes in the bed with me.
I know he hates me not.
I want everyone to see.

Victoria Hunter, Grade 3
Oak Park Elementary School, CA

My Life

First name Avery
Is caring, thinker, silly
Love sports, candy, thumper
Is good at gymnastics, video games, running
Feels happy, tired, joyful
Needs water, food, trees
Wants 3Ds, gold, ice cream
Fears failing, roaches, fire
Likes to eat crab, saimin, chicken
Watches Hawaii *Five-o*, *Glee*, *Angie's Garage*
Is a resident of Ewa Beach, Hawaii
Last name Chai

Avery Chai, Grade 3
Keone'ula Elementary School, HI

Ocean
Fish in the ocean,
swimming in colorful schools
bubbles around them.

Haley Gratz, Grade 3
McDowell Mountain Elementary School, AZ

Rainbows
Colorful rainbows.
Green wet clovers on the ground.
Cool soft breezes blow.

Marc DeNinis, Grade 3
McDowell Mountain Elementary School, AZ

Birds
They make me happy.
They are fat in the winter.
Birds fly like airplanes.

Trenton Bell, Grade 3
McDowell Mountain Elementary School, AZ

Dolphins
Dolphins sweet and cute.
Graceful creatures of the sea
Makes me so happy.

Domonique Varela, Grade 3
McDowell Mountain Elementary School, AZ

Light in Sight
Rain gushes down as it is gloomy and gray
Minutes later the rain stops
And light is in sight

Sam Kirley, Grade 2
Seattle Jewish Community School, WA

Squirrel
Squirrels scurrying
Up the trees and on the leaves
Yellow, orange, red, brown

Kaoru Hirayama, Grade 3
McDowell Mountain Elementary School, AZ

Thanksgiving

T urkey's in the oven for our feast.
H aving fun with my family.
A wonderful time with my family.
N ow time to have some fun.
K indness all around, put your frown upside down.
S aying our prayer before we have a Thanksgiving feast.
G od giving blessings for this holiday.
I smell turkey in the kitchen!
V ery exciting time on this holiday.
I eat yummy Thanksgiving food.
N ow getting ready to play games too!
G etting ready for our Thanksgiving feast.

Barbara Robinson, Grade 3
St John's Episcopal Day School, TX

The Tundra

The tundra may be old
but, it is quite cold.
There's lots of icebergs here and there
there's lot of icebergs everywhere.
It's warm in summer
but it's quite cold in winter.
There are animals on land
and there are animals in the ocean sand
but yet, I guess there's room for you and me
and everybody!
In the tundra, there is just so much to explore
I think the tundra is quite something to adore.

Jonathan Sautter, Grade 3
Goethe International Charter School, CA

Gazing at the Stars

If you gaze at the night sky, look for constellations.
You will see forms of many nations.
If you gaze at the night sky, look for the Big Dipper.
You will know what season we're in.
If you gaze at the night sky, look closely at the stars.
You will see interesting animals like Pegasus.
If you gaze at the night sky, look for planets.
You will see Venus after sunset.
So, whenever you gaze at the night sky, have an open mind.

Yusuf Amanullah, Grade 3
Islamic School of San Diego, CA

Chartreuse

Chartreuse is light green
Chartreuse is a slick color
Chartreuse is kind of dark
Chartreuse is crazy cool
Chartreuse tastes like mint chocolate
Chartreuse smells like minty flavors
Chartreuse sounds like nothing
Chartreuse feels like a light color on you
Chartreuse looks like a light green
Chartreuse makes me think about Joe (my dad)
Chartreuse is special to me because it was my dad's favorite color

Garcy LoCicero, Grade 1
Kentwood Elementary School, CA

Teachers

Teachers are great, teachers are fun,
I love every single one!

They teach you, encourage you, and make you strong,
They will never teach you anything that is wrong!

Some teach math, some teach science,
Anything they teach you will make sense!

They will make you very smart,
Teachers will always be in my heart!

Claudia Del Rio, Grade 3
St John's Episcopal Day School, TX

Pluto

What do the other planets think I am?
They used to be nice to me until two thousand six
Now they don't care about me —
I've been abused, abased, abandon.
And what about that Neptune trying to steal MY orbit?
Soon I'm going to crash into him,
and then I hope he learns his lesson.
One day I'm going to grow to be gargantuan
and decimate all of the other planets
like they tried to decimate me.
I feel like I have to scream — Aaaaahhhhhh!

Zachary Evans, Grade 3
Saigling Elementary School, TX

Homeward Bound

I'm on the bus, I'm going home.
The day is over, I am free
I did my homework, it was no work at all.
It's time to go, I really know.
The day is over, I've had the tests I did my best.
Saturday, here I come, you can't stop me
I am the best, just ask the rest.
I'm on the bus, I'm almost home.
I think I'll have a pop with chips.
Oh no, I'm last, I've missed my stop.
I'm on the bus, I'm going to school.
I hope they have a pool.

Asher Nederveld, Grade 3
Wilchester Elementary School, TX

About Me

First name Jordan
Is funny, smart, lazy
Loves dogs, family, God
Is good at video games, running, computers
Feels excited, playful, tired
Needs house, family, friends
Wants an iPhone, money, robot butler
Fears clowns, ghosts, the dark
Likes to eat chocolate, fish, pizza
Watches *Mad*, *Sponge Bob*, *Star Wars*
Is a resident of Ewa Beach, Hawaii
Last name Espenilla

Jordan Espenilla, Grade 3
Keone'ula Elementary School, HI

Christmas Is in the Air

You can smell it when the gingerbread cookies
come out of the oven.
You can taste it in the apple pie.
You can hear it when
Santa says ho, ho, ho.
You can see it when the
snow falls at night.
You can feel it when the
snow makes you cold.

David Baek, Grade 3
A E Arnold Elementary School, CA

Far to the West, Far to the East

Far to the west, far to the east,
There lies a bear hungry for food
Far to the west, far to the east,
A lonely man lays on a rocky mountain waiting
For the sun
Far to the west, far to the east,
An old sailor says, "Land Ho!"
Far to the west, far to the east,
10 cute kids roast marshmallows on a burning fire
Far to the west, far to the east,
I say, "The wilderness is a great place
to be."

Jamilee Jordan Rassy, Grade 3
Annunciation Orthodox School, TX

The Seaside

The shells at the beach are as shiny as a sparkling diamond
The seaweed is as green as clover from Ireland
The sea is as blue as the cloud-filled sky
The seagulls are as graceful as a colorful butterfly
The lobsters are as red as the fiery sun
People are jogging, going for a run
Sailboats are sailing on the rippling sea
Along with a warm summer breeze
Children are collecting sandy shells
People are laughing like tinkling bells
Sea snails are slithering, oozing slime
Everyone is having a wonderful time!

Isabella Lim, Grade 3
La Jolla Country Day School, CA

A Pencil Personality

I am a pencil named Anne.
I live in a cool, blue, big binder for old homework.
My favorite colors are bright green and red
because they are the colors of Christmas.
I like to wear thick and long pencil shavings.
My job is to write for my owner.
My family includes my brother Dan, my mom and my dad.
I go in journals for vacation.
My favorite holiday is Christmas because I get to hang out with family.

Anwesha Mukherjee, Grade 2
CLASS Academy, OR

High Merit Poems – Grades K, 1, 2, and 3

Blue Dance
I'm your whole world,
Wide and above you.
I am your whole world,
I spin around you.
Sirianna McLeod, Grade 3
Mount Pilchuck Elementary School, WA

Flowers
Flowers live at night.
Flowers love water and light.
They live with water and air
But they still look bare.
Esmeralda Lezo, Grade 2
St Helen Catholic School, CA

Copperhead Snakes
A Copperhead snake is poisonous.
It has a copper-colored head.
It has been found in the eastern
part of the U.S.A.
Cooper Patterson, Grade 2
Horn Academy, TX

Thanksgiving
Pumpkin pie with whipped cream
Cranberry sauce
Turkey and bread
Cranberry juice
Daniel Shetsky, Grade 1
Horn Academy, TX

Horses
Horses eat apples and grass
And run super fast
Babies don't know how
Till they are big.
Maya MacMillin, Grade 3
Goethe International Charter School, CA

My Mom
Nice
Beautiful
Kind
I love my mom!
Christopher Ho, Grade 1
Horn Academy, TX

Racing
Moving at a breaking speed
Everything is a blur
Hundreds of people screaming all day
I think I broke the sound barrier
Charlie Wilhite, Grade 3
Hewitt Elementary School, TX

My Cat
My cat is white
And he is black
He is my favorite cat
I love him so much
Chloe Saunders, Grade 1
Horn Academy, TX

The Boy in the Color Blue
The boy was blue
Because he had the flu.
The germs came to his body,
Because he was naughty.
Andrew Salas, Grade 2
St Helen Catholic School, CA

The Leaf
There is a leaf stuck on a tree.
There is a leaf waiting for me.
I climb up to the top branch.
Then the leaf falls straight in my hand.
Nathalie Keller, Grade 3
St Joseph Catholic School, CA

Little Creatures

Little creatures, little creatures.
I see little creatures.
I see them mostly everywhere.
'Cause they're just like little creepers.
They might be cute but they're everywhere!
I just might lose it!
Little creatures

Mary Grace McConn, Grade 3
Wilchester Elementary School, TX

Solar Radiation

The sun spits out solar radiation.
This radiation spews out of the sun at a rate of two million miles per hour.
January 23, 2012...
Remember how the sun let out its rage?
The burning ball kicked out something miniscule, but deadly.
Radiation as small as germs decimate and travel through space.
Beware...

Matteo Schneider, Grade 3
Saigling Elementary School, TX

Candy

Candy is good and sweet.
But sometimes sour.
It's sometimes hot or cold.
But it's still super good.
I like jelly beans, M&Ms, and Mike and Ikes.
But don't eat too much or you will be
sick. But soon you have to eat good food.

Alexander Van Kleek, Grade 3
Edward Byrom Elementary School, OR

Neptune

Nuclear Neptune is the god of the sea.
It's like ice — just two times more frozen.
This planet disguises itself like water,
but don't let the hydraulic gases fool you.
It's nitrogen!
This frozen planet is colder than an iceberg.
Brr! That's cold!

Nicholas Travis, Grade 3
Saigling Elementary School, TX

High Merit Poems – Grades K, 1, 2, and 3

Earth/Mars
Earth
Cold, hot
Moving, spinning, floating
Dog, cat, astronaut, craters
Moving, growing, floating
Hot, warm
Mars

Nathan Washington III, Grade 2
Tracy Learning Center - Primary Charter School, CA

The Easter Bunny
Hop, hope, here comes the Easter Bunny!
He bounces 24 hours a day!
The Easter bunny gives colored eggs to girls and boys.
The Easter bunny give chocolate chicks
and bubble gum candy to good girls and boys.
The Easter bunny is so awesome!
I love the Easter bunny!

Emma Grace Alexander, Grade 2
Annunciation Orthodox School, TX

My Shadow Friend
I have a nice and dark shadow friend
She does everything just like me
Like jumping, reading, eating, running, and being bright
But she only spends time with me in the light
I think my shadow friend's name is Annie
Do you think Annie saw the movie Bambi?
Well, Annie is always my shadow friend.

Emma Lowe, Grade 3
Speegleville Elementary School, TX

Cowboy
The happy cowboy was playing with children.
A rock band was playing.
The black midnight sky shining so bright.

The singing, so beautiful.
Then I could imagine that the rock band
wasn't a loud band.

Christian Cardona, Grade 3
H W Schulze Elementary School, TX

Stay Small for a While
Chubby little legs,
7 tooth smile,
Please stay this way,
Stay small for a while.
Hold my pinkie finger,
Suck on your bottle,
Do this forever,
Stay small for a while.

Kailey Morand, Grade 3
Darwin L Gilmore Elementary School, TX

Bowling
B alls are everywhere
O nly for fun to play
W in and have a good time
L ots of people play
I n lots of games you may score
N ot many people like it
G ames are only for fun

Ronin Tsang, Grade 2
Tracy Learning Center - Primary Charter School, CA

Forgive
Forgive, forgive
Do what Allah said.
Forgive, forgive, just forgive.
Forgive, forgive if someone punched you.
Please, please forgive.
You get good deeds if you forgive.
And you might go to Paradise if you forgive.

Eya Youssef, Grade 1
Islamic School of Muslim Educational Trust, OR

In the Desert
Some animals hide in their house
Such as owls, geckos, roadrunners,
A sand cat, a viper, and a kangaroo mouse.
In the desert
Animals hunt for food
Like a cactus beetle, Harris hawk, jerboa,
A Fennec fox, a cactus wren, and a red kangaroo.

Everett Morris, Grade 3
Goethe International Charter School, CA

High Merit Poems – Grades K, 1, 2, and 3

The Turquoise Ocean
The turquoise ocean is sparkling
under the sunset.
The sand is squishing
between my toes.
I feel the hot breeze
blowing across my face.
The ocean is wavier
than the wind.
The gray dolphins
jump like me
diving into the crystal water.
All in the turquoise ocean.
Charlie Douglas, Grade 2
Annunciation Orthodox School, TX

Hello Spring
Goodbye to blue and gray,
Hello to orange and pink.
I remember kids running,
And wanting a warm drink.
I remember it being bitter cold,
But now I sing and dance.
We used to throw snowballs,
But now we skip and prance.
Spring is finally here,
Winter is nowhere near,
So now I have nothing to fear,
Since spring is here.
Amanda Simpson, Grade 3
Woodway Elementary School, TX

Pencil
A pencil
is waiting to be sharpened.
It waits and it waits.
It tries to speak,
but the words can't come out.
Someone grabs the pencil.
They sharpen it.
Slowly,
it begins to die.
Vanessa Farias, Grade 2
Gause Elementary School, WA

Multnomah Falls
Powerful waterfall
splashes
into the lake.
People shouting
in delight.
Excited!
Excited!
Excited!
I wonder if anyone
is at Multnomah Falls now?
Happy!
Happy!
Happy!
Jackson Taylor, Grade 2
Gause Elementary School, WA

Thunder
Boom boom boom!
Sister is scared,
Hides under her bed,
Boom! Crash!
She cries loudly,
Hurts my ears
When crash, boom, crash!
Sister screams loudly
Until the lights
Flicker,
Everyone
Stays still
In silence.
Jimmy Amante IV, Grade 2
Robert L Stevens Elementary School, CA

Dogs
Dogs are big and little
Dogs have brown, black, and some white
Some have sand and some have mud
Dogs like to play catch
Dogs play with socks, shoes, and bones
I like all of the dogs
In the entire world!
Natalie Marklund, Grade 1
Horn Academy, TX

My Best Friend

My best friend ever
He watches us
He made everyone and everything
HE will never end
He is stronger than anything
I love Him
He made Earth
He made Heaven
He is God
Jorge Castillo, Grade 3
Legacy Christian Academy, NM

Blaine

Blaine
Nice, fast, happy
Loves baseball
Feels athletic
Needs better brothers
Gives friendship
Fears nothing
Would like to see Soak City
Stodder
Blaine Stodder, Grade 1
Kentwood Elementary School, CA

The Blue Sky

The sky is like water.
It shivers in the wind.
It moves like a snake.
The many different colors are beautiful.
It brightens the world
and makes the world shine.
Sadee Grace Neathamer, Grade 2
Gause Elementary School, WA

Winter

Snow is like sugar
falling from cotton candy clouds.
Snowflakes are dancing
quickly and quietly.
Oh, so sweet!
Emily Rabus, Grade 2
Gause Elementary School, WA

My Mom

I hear her heels.
I want her kisses.
I'm happy when she
takes me to Olive Garden.
I'm sad when she is crying.
I wish she could love me forever.
I believe she always watches over me.
I'm her daughter.
Miranda Villalobos, Grade 2
Vista Square Elementary School, CA

Astronauts

As their ship goes
Up into space
I watch it go
High it goes into
Space and
Then they come
Out to do research
On the moon
Jason Kuykendall, Grade 2
Horn Academy, TX

I Am Mad

I am mad
Very, very, very mad
When wind blows on me
I am still mad.
No one can stop me
From being mad
Because
I am mad!
Lucy Griffin, Grade 1
Horn Academy, TX

Cheetahs

Cheetahs are mammals,
They live in pods,
They are carnivorous,
They like to eat antelopes.
Cheetahs chase animals at night.
Karen Urbina, Grade 2
Mesa Vista Elementary School, TX

High Merit Poems – Grades K, 1, 2, and 3

School

School
is like
learning
at home.
Mom,
Dad,
brother,
aren't there.
Short days,
one recess,
long days,
two recesses.
Learning lots,
everything
is all perfect.
Kate Loya, Grade 2
Robert L Stevens Elementary School, CA

Inside a Library

When I go
in a library,
it sounds quiet,
I hear sounds of
books being taken out,
people whispering,
little kids,
and big kids,
having fun kids,
kids walking around,
moms saying
come here kids!
I am over there
in a corner
reading alone, quietly.
Yvette Pleites, Grade 2
Robert L Stevens Elementary School, CA

Things a Ferret Knows

What a ferret knows
How to scurry
How to scamper
How to hide in the hamper
How to bite
How to fight
How to run from the light
How to scratch
How to squeak
How to take a little peek
How to nibble
How to dribble
How to sneak the dogs
Kibble
This is what a ferret knows…squeak
Evan Heck, Grade 3
Spring Creek Elementary School, WY

Alone

Blue,
white,
bumpy,
hard,
football.
When I catch it, it hurts
Erik gets mad,
I'm alone.
No one
wants
to
play
with
me.
I'm alone.
Diego Diaz, Grade 2
Robert L Stevens Elementary School, CA

Clouds

Clouds move aimlessly
Drifting, beautiful
Fleecy, bringing welcome
Evan Padilla, Grade 3
Wilchester Elementary School, TX

Flowers

Sweet, scented
Delicate, fragile, soft
Colorful, bright, sunny, poppy
Vivi Cornell, Grade 3
Wilchester Elementary School, TX

Thankful

I am thankful for all my hands can hold —
The pencil that lets me write interesting stories when I'm bored.
My dad's warm hand that I can hold when I am scared.
My mom's hair that I can hold when I braid it.

I am thankful for all my eyes can see —
My mom who takes me to school,
My brother that cheers me up when I am sad,
The beautiful flowers that I can see when I pick them.

I am thankful for all my ears can hear —
The beautiful horse's neigh when I go to the barn,
The leaves that crackle when I step on them,
The water bottle crunch when I drink a lot of water.

I am thankful for all my mouth can taste —
My nana's turkey that I can eat when it is Thanksgiving
The yummy cookies that I make with my uncle at my grandma's house.

I am thankful for all my nose can smell —
The awesome yummy smell of cookies when I am special,
The scrumptious b-day cake when it is my birthday,
And the scented candles when I take a bath.

Chassidy Crittenden, Grade 3
A E Arnold Elementary School, CA

My Rabbit Lizzy

She feeds in the sunlight.
Eating the valuable carrot.
Hopping to a safe place to save,
The carrot from the parrot.

In the soft grass she nibbles.
Drinking from a bowl of fresh water.
She ate so much that she was,
At the bottom of the teeter totter.

Chewing on a big piece of salad.
Sitting on the smooth rock.
Eating ravenously in the garden.
Eating faster than the seconds on the clock.

Dana Bui, Grade 3
Oak Park Elementary School, CA

High Merit Poems – Grades K, 1, 2, and 3

Seal Summer
S ummer is fun.
E dges are laid down by seals.
A fter Ben was done surfing he was wet.
S urfing is cool but dangerous.
O nce Ben caught his breath he felt fine.
N ewly born seals are white.
Danny Benitez, Grade 3
Midland Elementary School, CA

The Shooting Star
The stars in the night
shine so bright
and the moon
is as bright as the sun.
The sun shines so
bright in the morning.
Brayden Boehm, Grade 3
Robinson Elementary School, TX

My Parents
My mom cooks and cleans the house.
She makes my hair in the morning.
My dad drops me off at school.
He works hard to get us money.
My parents love and care for me.
Safwa Khan, Kindergarten
Islamic School of San Diego, CA

Puppy
Puppy
Soft, cute
Running, sleeping, playing
Outside she feels sad
Dog
Brissa Fernandez, Grade 2
Meadows Elementary School, CA

Butterflies
Through the air they drift
Colorful wings take the sky
Floating gracefully
Zainab Zaman, Grade 2
Horn Academy, TX

Nothing Like You!
There is nothing like you.
You make me smile when there's
nothing to smile about.
You make everything fun when
nothing is fun.
You make nothing sad.
Until you died.
I love you, I miss you.
Maisey Herring, Grade 3
Robinson Elementary School, TX

Marine's Dream
I wish to be a Marine to fight for the
country in air and on land.
Any time to protect the country.
Whenever or wherever and to be
brave to fight day or night.
Until we win the fight and
when we do we will be part of the team.
Then wait for the next fight.
Drake Woodlee, Grade 2
Pleasanton Primary School, TX

I Wish I Could Meet Captain Hook
I wish I could meet Captain Hook
But he's only on T.V.
I think I can meet Captain Hook,
I just have to find out to see!
I hope Peter Pan won't mind
If not I've got to say
Oh, Peter Pan I'll get you for that
I'll get you for that someday!
Emalee David, Grade 2
Pleasanton Primary School, TX

Pets
Cute and loving pets
Fun, adorable puppies
Always your best friend
Dorothy Zhang, Grade 3
Medina Elementary School, WA

My Dad
Black, fuzzy hair with chocolate eyes,
In the hospital without me
And no one with me now,
Up, up and away now,
No one with me and sad.
Not breathing and missing him sadly.
Vanessa Guillen, Grade 2
Robert L Stevens Elementary School, CA

Hula Girl
I want to be a hula girl
Hula dance in
Skirts made of grass
Put fire on a stick
Twirl it like a baton
Sometimes surf with the dolphins!
Maria Muller, Grade 1
Johnson Elementary School, NV

Rainbow
Red is a rose
Blue is the sky
Yellow is a flower
Green is a superhero cape
Purple is grapes
Orange is a Halloween Jack-o-Lantern
Kevin Luc, Grade 1
CLASS Academy, OR

Clown
At the circus I saw clown.
On his face was a great big frown.
His sad eyes were big and brown.
Too bad, sad little clown.
Javan Cam Perryman, Grade 3
Robinson Elementary School, TX

Brave Dragon
Spikes on rough green wings
Flying through the big tough sky
Green rough wings flutter fast
Nicole Mao, Grade 2
Horn Academy, TX

Fantasy World
In a far far town
in a far far place
there is a place
called my fantasy
world.

In a faraway place
there is a waterfall
it streams down the
river of joy.

On the river of joy floats
a small gold coin.

On the small gold
coin is where my
story begins.

Everything happens
in my fantasy world.

It has
sunshine, rainbows,
clouds, and fun.
Madeline Reichel, Grade 3
Wilchester Elementary School, TX

Shapes
Rectangles have these...
4 sides and corners, you see,
opposite sides are the same.
Squares have these...
4 sides and corners, you see,
all are the same.
Circles have these...
no sides or corners, you see,
because they are round.
Triangles have these...
3 sides and corners, you see.
These are the shapes we learned in
geometry.
T. Amin's Kindergarten Class
Austin Peace Academy, TX

Thanksgiving

T urkey
H as
A lways been our
N ation's favorite
K ind of
S ubject when we are
G iving thanks
I n our blessings like the
V ery thankful Pilgrims and
I ndians of our
N ation. Pilgrims and Indians are known for
G iving thanks.

Wiley Melcher, Grade 3
Wilchester Elementary School, TX

Glimmering Snowflakes

Glimmering stars pirouetting, silent as night
Silver bells falling from the sky in a gentle wind
Crystals dancing in a quiet night
Miniature silk ribbons swirling through the day
Gentle raindrops shining in the air, like Santa coming to my house
Elegant flowers swaying throughout the world
Little butterflies gracefully flying towards the ground
Exquisite ballerinas spiraling like petals in a wedding
Christmas lights twinkling at midnight
Glistening gumdrops falling from the clouds
Little embroidery sewn in the air
Angels climbing from the Heavens

Alaina Cruson, Grade 3
Lolo Elementary School, MT

Rain

Rain drops dripping, drip-drop, drip-drop
Rain drops splashing, splish-splosh, splish-splosh
Tears of water.
Jump in the rain,
Play in the rain,
Dance in the rain.
Sun comes out,
A rainbow.

Nicolas, Annabella, Gabby, Kennedy, McKenna, Julia Sandoval, and Will
Kindergarten
The Presentation School, CA

The Song for Mother Nature
Do you hear the birds
singing in front of Mother Nature
And watching us until we go to heaven?
Jesus loves us forever
Nature is beautiful

Esperanza Gracious Romero, Kindergarten
Mosaic Academy Charter School, NM

Index

Abawe, Grace 123
Abdalla, Sofia 21
Abdul-Alim, Lubnaa 83
Abitante, Brett 12
Able, Connor 112
Aceituno, Audrey 110
Acosta, Isabella E. 83
Adkins, Everett 123
Aeschlimann, Gabrielle . 81
Agarwal, Aseem 60
Agha, Joseph 64
Aguilar, Gabriela 80
Ahmad, Nafees 66
Ahmed, Nawar 86
Ajawara, Kelechi 68
Al-Bawani, Salma 119
Alcazar, Sophia 120
Alexander, Aubrey 37
Alexander, Emma Grace 145
Alexander, Silja 108
Allen, Natalie 131
Allred, Jackson 16
Almakky, Danyal 66
Alvarez, Alexis 92
Amante IV, Jimmy 147
Amanullah, Yusuf 139
Amin, T. Amin's
    Kindergarten Class .. 152
Anaya-Morford,
    Annaliese 87
Annabella 153
Anderson, Jonathan 83
Anderson, Kiana 80
Anesi, Corey 79
Anoai, Vaughan 24
Arellano, Hannah 76
Arend, Drew 71
Arevalo, Daniella 47
Arevalo, Isabella 19
Armenta, Alondra 70

Arntzen, Wade 42
Arya, Arman 34
Ash, Alexi 111
Ashley, Caroline 27
Austin, Kaylom 17
Ava 89
Awad, Reem 109
Ayers, Sequoia 133
Badger, Maddie 27
Baek, David 141
Bailey, Jordin 8
Bailey, Sasha 127
Banaga, Ricardo 14
Banda, Vincent 77
Barnes, Jazmin 10
Barragan, Jovanni 20
Bartley, Alexis 10
Barve, Noopur 134
Bashir, Sarah 88
Bechky, Aviva 38
Becker, Kai 93
Begay, Rakeem 71
Begaye, Randal 33
Bell, Trenton 138
Benally, Cheyenne 71
Benavidez, Aaliyah 21
Benitez, Danny 151
Bennett, Rudy 126
Bhansali, Rohan 9
Bhat, Aaditya 20
Boehm, Brayden 151
Boersma, Ainsley 104
Bolger, Kate 10
Borucki, Jenna 106
Boukouzis, Tess 46
Bragg, Berkley 126
Breanna 40
Brenner, Hanna 80
Bright, Aidan 43
Brittain, Vivian 14

Brokaw, Shade 38
Bronk, Annaka-Joy 94
Brooks, Elanah 62
Brooksby, Britain 66
Brooksby, Sydney 10
Brown, Ed 82
Brown, Emma 78
Brown, Gunnar 131
Bui, Dana 150
Burkett, Kathleena 103
Burnham, Bridger 90
Burson, Shilo 74
Bury, Jordan 17
Byun, Aaron 43
Cadman, Kayleigh 71
Cain, Michayla 39
Cambridge, Dominic 71
Campbell, Saylor 111
Cannon, Cadee 90
Canon, Sage 10
Cardona, Christian 145
Cariaso, Alyzai 18
Carlos, Kyle 104
Carrasco, Lilia 61
Carrillo, Madelyn 111
Cashio, Logan 25
Casias, Dristen 118
Castellano, Chris 12
Castillo, Jorge 148
Castro, Emma 132
Caveness, Aidyn 27
Cha, Jimin 14
Chai, Avery 137
Chan, Cassandra 35
Chance, Madelyn 123
Chang, Zoe 23
Chavez, Rodolfo 57
Chen, Brian 62
Chen, Edward 51
Chen, Katherine 12

A Celebration of Poets – West Grades K-3 Spring 2012

Chen, Preston 33
Chen, Zoe 81
Chesney, John 56
Chetty, Rushil 18
Chiquet Torres, Jocelyne 124
Chow, Tobias 28
Clark, Azeza 107
Clark, Caroline 124
Classen, Ella 48
Clawson, Kayden 64
Claypool, Claire 22
Cloud, Cody 52
Cohen, Sam 16
Colabianchi, Brandon ... 93
Colvin, Aiden 92
Conn, Ariana 98
Conner, Marshall 116
Connerty, Tess 30
Conway, Ellie 70
Cooler, Dillon 90
Corbin, Evan 111
Cornell, Vivi 149
Corona, Andrew 96
Cortes, Roberto 28
Cortez, Makyla 60
Crittenden, Chassidy 150
Cronin, Nicole 110
Cruse, Ava 67
Cruson, Alaina 153
Cui, Jonathan 98
Dang, Catherine 28
Dannenberg, Drake 93
David, Emalee 151
Davidson, Oliver 123
Davine, Alice 69
Deas, Kamal 88
Deb, Aakanksha 132
DeCamp, David 40
Deer, Airey 30
Deere, Braidon 17
Del Rio, Claudia 140
DeNinis, Marc 138
Dering, Sidney 64
DeSoto, Caden 90
Dessens, Kyle 42
Dex, Sophia 120

Dhadiala, Sukhmani 53
Dhillon, Harleen 56
Diaz, Diego 149
Dibble, Kayden 80
Dina, Caroline 9
Dingman, Colton 54
DiPaolo, Joelle 88
Dixon, Carter 94
Dopp, Reagan 120
Douglas, Charlie 147
Dowell, Katheryn 127
Doyle, Alexa 136
Dozal, Benjamin 19
DuBois, William 39
Dunbar, Rommel 62
Duxbury, Gavin 52
Earley, Mia 25
Eaton, Max 18
Echeverria, Sophia 43
Efron, Samuel 83
Eldegwy, Omar 103
Emerson, Maya 65
Emery, Caroline 129
Endres, Ella 75
Erriche, Fatima 114
Escobedo, Jose 63
Espenilla, Jordan 141
Esquivel, Mia 126
Estrada, Yadel 121
Evans, Zachary 140
Faaborg, Paige 116
Fairchild, Jasper 90
Faks, Muhammad 78
Farah, Sara 66
Farias, Vanessa 147
Farnum, Neeley 18
Feeney, Lucy 22
Ferguson, Joelle 14
Fernandez, Brissa 151
Fernandez, Marcelo 81
Finnegan, Evan 59
Fitjar, Sebastian 18
Fittipaldi, Bruno-Nicolas 50
Fitzgerald, Miles 40
Flores, Aaliyah 93
Flores, America 48

Flores, Mirna 69
Fontanez, Mikail 135
Fortenberry, Macy 24
Fox, Camden 33
Frediani, Angelina 53
French, Orrin 27
Fritze, Tyson 20
Frush, Madison 136
Gaballo, Anthony 101
Gabby 153
Gadbois, Ethan 132
Galimi, Hunter 113
Gao, David 26
Garcia, Alexandria 31
Garcia, Ayleen 106
Garcia, David 59
Garcia, Luis 125
Garza, Madyson 92
Gayrard, Caitlyn 33
Gebbia, Mysteri 72
Gillette, Makenzie 94
Goddard, Samuel 86
Golden, Collin 133
Goldenberg, Abigail 75
Gomez, Derek 83
Gonzales, Arianna 29
Gonzalez, Nathanial 20
Gonzalez, Neomi 74
Goodell, Ethan 92
Gottesman, Cayla 12
Graham, Callum 29
Gratz, Haley 138
Gray, Kirby 35
Greene, Danielle 39
Greenlee, Timia 33
Griffin, Lucy 148
Griffiths, Grant 111
Grobler, Genevieve 22
Guerrero, Fernando 51
Guikema, Augustus 103
Guillen, Vanessa 152
Gurtzweiler, Elijah 51
Guzman, Sylvana 16
Habib-Dueben, Sophia 135
Hada, Kate E. 131
Haegner, Jake 67

Index

Hakanen, Emily 27
Hall, Jalan 72
Hallmark, Mia................ 42
Hamilton, Trenton 135
Hancock, Hunter........... 65
Haratsu, Yuta 34
Harger, Cade.................. 34
Harris, Georgia.............. 50
Hatch, Sydney 52
Hays, Cody 116
Heatherington, Hailey ... 51
Heck, Evan 149
Hedrick, Jonathan.......... 36
Helmy, Ibrahim............ 113
Helpert, Colton.............. 95
Henderson, Ajah............ 72
Hernandez, Dalila.......... 74
Hernandez, Jose 98
Hernandez, Junior 43
Hernandez, Maximiliano 27
Hernandez, Zoe 92
Herrera, Arielle.............. 70
Herrera, Carlos............. 113
Herring, Maisey............ 151
Hester, Callie 21
Hester, Kate................... 51
Hickman, Emma............ 50
Hirayama, Kaoru 138
Ho, Christopher........... 143
Hochglaube, Quinn 50
Horton, Jonathan Daniel . 9
Hoskie, Tisheena 17
Hoskison, Jonathon 90
Hsu, Leo........................ 33
Hsu, Veronica 121
Hua, Joseph 107
Huang, Franklin 92
Huffman, Philip 32
Hughes, Lily 48
Hunter, Victoria........... 137
Hutchins, Warren........... 95
Huynh, Vivian 16
Ikeda, James 105
Ikeda, Joshua 98
Imran, Shaheer 21
Interian, Sahily.............. 25

Jacky, Richard 129
Janousek, Alexis 114
Jeffery, Joseph 98
Jeffries, Ella 10
Jegi, Sophia 114
Jerde, Evelyn................. 85
Jin, Oceana.................... 67
Jobe, Amelia 13
Johnny, Monnie............. 28
Johnson, Jaden 36
Johnson, Savannah........ 75
Johnston, Demi 48
Jones, Joygavion........... 132
Jones, Kierra.................. 71
Jones, Mason 16
Jones, Wylie 35
Josephson, Violet........... 58
Judy, Oren..................... 51
K., Harlie 22
Kamel, Mariana 46
Kamran, Izzah 23
Kant, Grace 20
Kastner, Gigi................ 104
Kavvy 89
Kazden, Joshua 18
Keeble, Caleb 25
Keeler, Trenton.............. 43
Keller, Nathalie 143
Kennedy 153
Keohohou, Joshua.......... 40
Khan, Ali..................... 117
Khan, Safwa 151
Kimzey, James 50
King, Keienna................ 71
Kirillov, Maxim 126
Kirley, Sam 138
Klasing, Keaton 34
Konings, Iza Rae.......... 136
Koo, Joyce..................... 55
Krishnan, Sharad............ 8
Ku, Claire 121
Kumar, Ishani.............. 122
Kumar, Trishna............ 110
Kuykendall, Jason 148
Kwiatkowski,
 Katarzyna V. 109

Lambert, Kaelen........... 134
Lang, Brock................... 51
Lang, Sasha................... 36
Larios-Chacon,
 Alma Xotchitl 38
Larson, Ireland 90
Lasater, Alex 34
Lavorini, Jacob.............. 50
Lazo, Zoila.................... 50
Leather, Payton 17
Lee, Lawrence............... 56
Lee, Regina.................... 65
Lee, Suzanne................ 127
Lemersal, Henry............ 26
Lenchitsky, David 68
Levi, Matalina 130
LeWarne, Nicolas 45
Lewin, Zachary............ 110
Lezo, Esmeralda 143
Li, Alan 94
Li, Henry..................... 129
Liao, Sydney 91
Licona, Dayshell 135
Lim, Isabella 142
Lind, Catalina 135
Lipitz, Chloe 49
Lipps, Zoey.................... 77
List, Savannah 44
Liu, Nerissa 120
Livingstone, Mateo......... 16
LoCicero, Garcy........... 140
Locke, Elianah............... 95
Lomban, Karissa 25
Longoria, Angelina 99
Lonial, Diya.................. 77
Lonsdale, Emily 93
Loo, Brandon 49
Lopez, Brooklyn 95
Lopez, Gaynell............... 88
Love, Kylen 10
Lowe, Emma 145
Loya, Kate................... 149
Luc, Kevin................... 152
Lucero, Ashlan 32
Luna, Lexi 38
Lyons, Faith.................. 25

A Celebration of Poets – West Grades K-3 Spring 2012

MacDonald, Donovan.. 114
MacGregor, William..... 115
Mackenzie, Jennifer....... 24
MacMillin, Maya 143
Magana, Armando 49
Mah-Bishop, Madysen . 129
Maldonado, Jenna.......... 91
Maldonado, Madellyn.... 81
Malin, Dana 11
Mandeville-Martinez, Isabella................. 101
Mandeville-Martinez, Vicente..................... 80
Mao, Nicole 152
Marchand, Abryanna... 108
Marchi, Liam 39
Mariano, Vydazia 71
Marin, Valerie............... 119
Mark............................... 89
Marklund, Natalie........ 147
Markowitz, Jonathan 89
Martin, Jordin 110
Martinez, Brianna 9
Martinez, Salvador 53
Martinez III, Noel 111
Masterfield, Hailey 74
Matchers, Courtney........ 17
Matthew, Rhett............... 52
May, Brooklyn 74
Mazon, Charlize........... 102
McCall, Ryan................ 112
McCarthy, Maggie 82
McConn, Mary Grace ... 144
McConnell, Caitlyn 127
McDonald, Steven 113
McElroy, Kaydon 38
McGee, Elizabeth 122
McKenna 153
McLeod, Sirianna......... 143
McMahon, Lilly 103
McMahon, Lindsey....... 108
Meka, Sashank............. 128
Melcher, Wiley............. 153
Mersereau, Olivia........... 67
Messina, Jeanette 110
Mills, Drake 29

Mills, George 16
Minear, Roman 60
Miner, Danny 82
Molander, Abigaile 96
Monfiero, Alyssa........... 127
Monroe, Cole 12
Mora, Muriel 69
Mora, Wayo 135
Morand, Kailey............. 146
Moreno, Genesis............ 68
Morris, Everett............. 146
Mota, Hailey 41
Mota, Laura.................... 40
Motes, Madison 98
Mukherjee, Anwesha... 142
Muller, Maria 152
Munger, Matthew 106
Munn, Matt 48
Myers, Jayden 89
Nadery, Lyda.................. 36
Nair, Roshen.................. 98
Naki-Kanamu, Skye..... 125
Nam, Aaron 86
Nates, Leore................... 34
Nathan, Aviva............... 117
Naveen, Amreen 99
Nayak, Nikhil 67
Nayvelt, Kaila 86
Neathamer, Sadee Grace 148
Nederveld, Asher 141
Neff, Gideon 90
Nellen, Hannah.............. 98
Newstadt, Joseph 12
Neyoy, Italia 49
Nguyen, Alexander......... 21
Nguyen, Jadelyn 41
Nguyen, Victoria 97
Nguyen, Vivian 102
Nicolas......................... 153
Nomani, Moin Uddin..... 24
Nors, Hannah................. 24
Ocampos, Anya.............. 94
Oechsner, Emilee 96
Olbekson, Caden 34
Olivarez, Angelo 118

Olivas, David 71
Onesti, Dean................... 25
Ontiveros, Alondra......... 48
Ordorica, Stephen........ 118
Orosco, Madalynn.......... 76
Ortega-Portillo, Michael 84
Outley, Nigel.................. 78
Padilla, Evan................ 149
Padilla, Patrick 100
Palmerton, Austin.......... 11
Pannu, Gurshaan 107
Parker............................ 89
Parnell, Cade................ 117
Parnell, Caroline.......... 112
Patterson, Cooper 143
Patton, Jenna 117
Paul, Genevieve.............. 45
Paz, Jade........................ 43
Pedarla, Kusal.............. 127
Pelican, Alaina............. 122
Pellegrino, Sophia 119
Pena, Izaya.................... 30
Perez, Samantha............ 97
Perkins, Torin 9
Perryman, Javan Cam . 152
Pham, Brandon 81
Pham, Catherine.......... 104
Phillips, Kate................. 77
Phillips, Madison 40
Piazza, Jason................. 53
Piazza, Madison........... 109
Pieper, Olivia............... 133
Pierznik, Richelor.......... 67
Pinkstaff, Drew 135
Pitcher, Caleb................ 43
Pittsenbarger, Jacob..... 104
Pleites, Yvette 149
Polyakovsky, Edee 74
Ponteres, Jamie 14
Powell, Brenna............... 67
Powers, Kaitlin............. 123
Prasad, Haley 11
Quintana-Sanchez, Despina 84
Quintana-Sanchez, Valentina 24

Index

Rabus, Emily 148
Ramali, Damien 14
Ramayla, Richard 100
Ramesh, Nisarga 105
Ramirez, Alejandra 33
Ramirez, Aylissia 117
Ramirez, Reese 134
Ramirez, Roman 67
Ramirez, Sabrina 55
Ramos, Russell 11
Ramos, Xavier 126
Randle, Olivia 85
Rangel, Karina 17
Rasheed, Mostafa 32
Rasmussen, McKinzie 68
Rassy, Jamilee Jordan .. 142
Rathgeber, Kody 11
Raveendranath, Ranjani 69
Rawa, Ashley 38
Ray, Emily Grace 14
Raz, Tristan 121
Reddy, Ramya 73
Reed, Hunter 52
Reeves, Brian 113
Reichel, Madeline 152
Reyes, Ernie 33
Rich, Julian 16
Richardson, Kade 34
Richter, Jaidyn 67
Riordan, John 110
Rios, Hailey 25
Rios, Shaun Scott 21
Rios, Steve 43
Rishikesan, Sanjita 73
Robb, Peyton 22
Roberts, Jyla 69
Robinson, Barbara 139
Rocha, Armando 47
Roche, Caroline 119
Rodriguez, Gabriela 18
Rodriguez, Kevin 10
Rodriguez, Maximiliano 64
Roehrig, Tyberious 104
Rojas, Maria 16
Romero,
   Esperanza Gracious 154

Rubio, Amanda 50
Rubio, Lucas 42
Rueda, Samantha 80
Rump, Avery 61
Sachdeva, Miles 69
Sadiarin, Sydney 31
Saether, David 86
Saiz, Miranda 62
Salas, Andrew 143
Salazar, Jordan 101
Saldaña, Edward 96
Samii, Ayden 41
Samp, Abbie 35
Sandadi, Vinutha 54
Sandoval, Julia 153
Sandoval, Thabita 136
Santiago, Alyssa 124
Santiago-Mendez, Karla 74
Santoya, Naydean 57
Sarkar, Mohor 14
Saunders, Chloe 143
Sautter, Jonathan 139
Saxena, Krishna 64
Scheland, Will 94
Schmalz, Jase 98
Schmalz, Jennifer 28
Schmedthorst, Hunter . 111
Schneider, Matteo 144
Scholz, Mikayla 80
Schumann, Gelina 56
Scott, Natalie 105
Sehorn, Whitley 48
Serpas, Emily 51
Sexauer, Zoe 113
Sgouros,
   Emmanuel George.... 23
Sgouros, Zoe 109
Shah, Kavi 24
Shanley, Conor 18
Shannon, Faith 39
Sharpe, Rhys 54
Shaw, Alison 73
Shaw, Elijah 53
Shaw, Hailey 122
Shea 89
Shek, Jocelyn 85

Shetsky, Daniel 143
Shetty, Rohan 76
Shim, Eubin 136
Short, Jalen 75
Shull, Jenna 110
Siciliano, Benjamin 98
Siciliano, Nathan 61
Siddiqah, Fatimah 99
Siddiqui, Maryam 55
Silver, Chloe 44
Simpson, Amanda 147
Simpson, Katherine 135
Sims, Caleb 21
Sims, Kagan 64
Singamsetty, Vinay 126
Singh, Devak 120
Skeet, Renae 113
Slim, Shane 90
Smith, Alexander 121
Smith, Allison 90
Smith, Christian 56
Soltanovich, Eric 22
Sood, Aditya 75
Sorce, Olivia 130
Sotello, Jazelle 87
Soto, Alex 57
Sousa, Isabella 115
Spadachene, Aubrey 96
Spears, Blaine 120
Sridhar Baskari,
   Aadithyaa 15
Sriram, Keerthi 20
Stankowski,
   Mia Katherine 57
Statiras, Nikolas 74
Steen, Caroline 40
Stellino, Nicholas 17
Stephens, Tyrus 79
Stevens, Tony 126
Stinson, Cha-Cha 84
Stodder, Blaine 148
Storey, Gillian 107
Storms, Tipanga 45
Stribling, Isabel 67
Stuckey, Matthew 86
Suell III, Doug 15

Sullivan, Daniel 97
Summerfield, Kaylia 38
Sverdlov, Sarah 87
Swanston, Sophia 74
Sweet, Parker 66
Syed, Hana 13
Syed, Ilyas 48
Talia 89
Tang, Arthur................ 117
Tashiro, Hikaru.............. 68
Tatro-Humphreys,
    Sienna 29
Taylor, Cylar 28
Taylor, Jackson 147
Taylor, Peyton 117
Tellez, Annie.................. 16
Tenbroeke, Christopher . 95
Terry, Avery.................... 27
Teswood, Rachelle.......... 71
Thaller, Maggie 61
Thange, Hamza............ 116
Thilgen, Craig.................. 9
Thomas, Nesto 117
Tolentino, Angela........... 11
Tomas, Isabella............ 113
Toomes, Kylie 78
Torres, Frankie............... 96
Toumi, Ayoub 8
Tovar, Abigail 37
Trad, Tony 130
Trammell, Sophie 115
Tran, Maggie 24
Tratt, Shai 75
Travis, Nicholas............ 144
Trilling, Ava.................. 117
Tsang, Ronin................ 146
Tsigos, Helena 87
Tucker, Cody.................. 59
Tucker, Giovanni............ 33
Tucker, Penelope.......... 120
Tucker, Wyatt............... 100
Tuite, Ryan 80
Urbina, Karen 148
Uribe, Alexandra 113
Usmani, Ebaad............... 95
Valdivia, Bianca 17

Van Den Berg, Breawna 128
Van Kleek, Alexander ... 144
Varela, Domonique 138
Velasquez, Deandra....... 63
Velasquez, Isabel 15
Vestal, Molly 18
Vierra, Maggie............. 102
Villalobos, Miranda...... 148
Villanueva, Ariel............ 68
Viswanathan, Rhea...... 111
Voss, ShayLynn.............. 83
Wakefield, Emma........... 94
Walthers, Beck............... 64
Wang, Vicky................... 44
Washington, Cameron... 99
Washington III, Nathan 145
Weatherby, Robert......... 51
Weiss, Carrie.................. 63
Wellington, Karris.......... 83
West, Meera 115
Wheeler, Anthony.......... 32
Whitehead, Amanda 78
Whitton, Will................. 11
Wilhite, Charlie............ 143
Wilkins, Mark Austin 82
Will.............................. 153
Williams, Emma 113
Williams, Isabella 42
Williams, Karis............... 61
Willie, Daytral 31
Willim, Lance.............. 112
Wilson, Morgan............. 35
Wise, Laken 49
Wolfe, Kaia.................. 127
Wolfe, Sydney................ 77
Woodlee, Drake 151
Woolbright, Foster......... 93
Wright, Jalen 83
Wyble-Ceno, Joseph....... 23
Wylie, Ava 112
Xu, Kristin 34
Yamaguchi, Patrick 125
Yanke, Julia 129
Yarbrough, Natalia 92
Yates, Melodie................ 89
Yazzie, Kacie.................. 96

Ye, Katherine 44
Yonemura, Jeremiah...... 69
Young, Katherine 34
Youngquist, Kyle 86
Youssef, Eya................. 146
Yu, Emily....................... 18
Yu, Jacob..................... 119
Zaman, Zainab............. 151
Zamora, Marco 88
Zatarain, Melody............ 17
Zermeno, Santi 58
Zhang, Dorothy............ 151
Zhang, Nina 35
Zhu, Sernry 86
Zohnnie, Regan 96
Zuniga, Daitlyn 128
Zurek, Niko 117